SECRETS & LIES

ELITE FIGHTING UNITS

SECRETS & LIES

ELITE FIGHTING UNITS

EXPOSING THE TRUTH BEHIND HISTORY'S MOST LETHAL FIGHTERS

HOWARD WATSON

METRO BOOKS
New York

METRO BOOKS
New York

Publisher: Sarah Bloxham
Quantum Editorial: Sam Kennedy and Hazel Eriksson
Production Manager: Rohana Yusof
Design: Amazing 15

ISBN 978-1-4351-5481-0

For information about custom editions, special sales, and premium and corporate purchases,
please contact Sterling Special Sales at 800-805-5489 or specialsales@sterlingpublishing.com.

Manufactured in China by 1010 Printing International Ltd.

2 4 6 8 10 9 7 5 3 4

www.sterlingpublishing.com

Contents

Introduction

FROM THE 300 Spartan hoplites who defied the Persian hordes at Thermopylae, to the SAS soldiers storming the Iranian Embassy, or Navy SEAL Team 6 appearing out of the sky to dispatch Osama bin Laden, many of the most inspiring, surprising, and momentous military feats have been performed by fighting elites. And obscuring the facts, activities, tactics, and techniques of every elite fighting unit sprawls a web of secrets and lies.

Throughout history, unique units of highly trained soldiers have specialized in fighting against the odds, performing operations that many would deem foolhardy, and using unconventional tactics to defeat the enemy. The history of the fighting elite is littered with tales of men courageously putting their lives on the line in the pursuit of valor, in the name of a cause, or just because they were born to fight.

An elite is a group of people considered to be the superior part element of a society or organization, in this case within the broader military establishment. Yet being a specialized small unit in a broader army is not enough to be an elite. From the 300 Spartans in the 5th century BC to the United States' Delta Force in the 21st century the bands of fighters featured in this book share other special factors that have made them stand out from all the rest.

Every military elite is created for a special purpose, which often means that their actions must remain secret. In ancient history, the elite role was often to act as the leader's personal bodyguard, protecting him and, by extension, the state from harm, whether it is dealt by the hand of enemy forces abroad or political rivals at home. Elites would also undertake secretive, specialized roles within battle, performing innovative maneuvers or acting as a shock force sent into battle at a crucial moment. These days, with the rise of global terrorism, the purpose of the elite is rarely to take part in full-scale battle: instead, it often involves covert operations behind enemy lines, counter-terrorism, hostage situations, and insertion and extraction missions in foreign territories. The need for secrecy has never been greater.

To perform these special functions, loyalty is essential. With loyalty comes resoluteness, without which military units—when facing terrible odds—will simply throw down their arms and surrender. This loyalty is twofold: there is loyalty to the broader cause, whether it be political, religious, national, or ethnic; and—crucially—there is loyalty to the unit itself.

On the battlefield or in the heat of a covert operation, it is often that second type of loyalty that makes soldiers perform the impossible. The unit is a band of brothers, united by their fellowship, their company insignia, uniform, traditions, code, and motto: they are spurred on to fight for each other, having shared successes and endured hardships both in training and in battle. Sometimes a shared ethnicity fosters this internal loyalty; witness the Viking Varangians, the Polish lancers of Napoleon, and the Gurkhas of the British. In one case, the Sacred Band of Thebes, the unit was bound together by love. Being a body of fighting men—a *corps d'elite*—does not suffice; to be effective the unit must be also have an *esprit de corps*, a common spirit of comradeship and a willingness to die for each other. Soldiers, or operators as they have increasingly become known, are often sworn to secrecy about a unit's activities, even after they have left the force: they must not reveal information which puts their fellow soldiers at risk.

In the best units, the *esprit de corps* becomes ingrained through the tough, rigorous, highly disciplined, and secret training routines, which help develop two other essential features of the military elite: endurance and skill. From the Spartans to the SAS, recruits are tested to the utmost to see whether they can endure the travails of the campaign or operation. Strength and stamina, both physical and mental, are vital, as is the ability to survive on foreign shores without proper rations or back-up. Endurance was key to the success of Rogers' Rangers on the St. Francis Raid, to Merrill's Marauders in their horrendous mission into the jungles of Burma, to the Green Berets working behind enemy lines in Vietnam, and to modern special operations forces, often deposited for covert, long-range, isolated missions in enemy-occupied territory. That endurance extends to interrogation: whatever tortures a

captured elite soldier must endure, he must keep the unit's secrets, protecting them from exploitation by the enemy.

Specialist skills, of course, have always been a major factor of the elite—from the swordsmanship of the samurai to the marksmanship of the Streltsy—but they have become even more prevalent in the modern era. Today, forces are trained to the utmost in the execution of maneuvers, the use of secret new technology and weaponry, reconnaissance and surveillance techniques, sabotage, close quarter combat, and marksmanship. Often the skill-set must extend to stealth operations such as airborne or amphibious insertions, where specialist parachuting and combat swimming capabilities are essential.

However, a loyal, highly trained, expert marksman able to survive undercover for weeks at a time would be better off working as a desk clerk if he lacked courage. This is the base component of the elite soldier. The successful elites in this book are marked out by their willingness to die for their cause; to do more than the average soldier; to try to defeat the enemy even when grossly outnumbered or cornered. The bravura of the 300 men at Thermopylae is no different from that shown by the Navy SEALs today: they put their lives on the line to do what other men would regard as mission impossible.

Amongst all the tales of derring-do found in the pages of this book, there is also a dark seam running through the history of the fighting elite. Some

elites, such as the Praetorian Guards of Rome, become self-important and loyal only to their own secret agenda: they can end up as power-brokers, king-makers, and even assassins, playing with the future of the state. Some elites became military anachronisms; having become engorged with power, they refused to advance in military terms. The Streltsy and the Janissaries became concerned only for their own rights and objectives, and, fatally, refused to adapt to advances in military techniques and strategies. They became bloated, treasury-sapping armies that, through their political gamesmanship, were a great threat to their own leaders, but little danger to the enemy in military terms. Consequently, they had to go.

The best elites manage to adapt to modern warfare and stay true to their role as soldiers protecting the state. Whatever the politics, their intention remains the same: to be the best; to go the extra mile; to show courage, valor, bravery, and supreme skill, whatever the situation, whatever the number of the opposition, whatever the danger.

The good and bad qualities of the fighting elite make every unit described here fascinating. One thing is for sure: in an age where full field battles are becoming an irrelevance, unconventional fighting elites and their covert activities are becoming ever more important in the modern age. And every tale is full of secrets …

THE FEARLESS SPARTAN WARRIORS

300

The loyal brotherhood of citizen-soldiers who sacrificed themselves at the Battle of Thermopylae

IN 480 BC just 300 Spartans stood against 150,000 Persians at the Battle of Thermopylae. They been trained to fight—and die—for their cause ever since they were young children. And die they did, every single one of them, as they were unwilling to lay down their shields even in the face of such impossible odds.

True Spartans, known as Spartiates, were allowed just one profession—soldier—and they took that role more seriously than any other citizens of the warring city-states of Ancient Greece. National service in modern countries usually lasts for one or two years. In Sparta it lasted for 40 years.

The Spartan regime was so tough that the word "Spartan" has entered the English dictionary as shorthand for fearlessness, austerity, and harshness. The ideal of the Spartan army was created by the philosopher Lycurgus in the 8th century BC. The war-mongering city-states of Ancient Greece were usually surrounded by high walls for protection, but Lycurgus wanted to create "a wall of men, not of bricks." This wall of men was made up of Spartiate hoplites—citizen-soldiers, not mercenaries or slaves. Under Lycurgus' direction, the whole of Spartan

FACT FILE

REGION: Ancient Greece
ERA: 8th century to 2nd century BC
KEY ENCOUNTERS: Battle of Thermopylae 480 BC; Battle of Platea 479 BC; Peloponnesian War 431–404 BC; Battle of Leuctra 371 BC
TACTICS AND TECHNIQUES: Highly specialized military training from childhood; disciplined infantry fighting in phalanx formation
WEAPONRY: Shield, javelin, long spear, short sword
LEGACY: Originated new era of military training; known for bravery against the odds

society became military-oriented in pursuit of the values of austerity, strength, fitness, democracy, and equality. Like so many later elites, the secret to the success of the Spartan army was that they were a highly trained, disciplined, and loyal brotherhood who would die for one another.

The training regime of the Spartiates was merciless. At birth, a baby boy would be inspected by the Gerousia, the council of elders. If he was deemed to be weak or deformed he was simply left on a mountainside to die from exposure. Boys who were healthy and strong were taken from their mothers at the age of seven and sent to the Agoge, the military training school, where they would live in barracks.

Spartan boys usually went naked until the age of 12, when they were allocated a red cloak, which they would wear whatever the season. It became their uniform. They were also given an older Spartiate mentor who would train them in the secrets of the Spartan military. Unlike the

Right: A Spartan soldier bearing his prized shield

neighboring city-state of Athens, Sparta did not prize all-round education. The boys were taught to read, but there was little desire to match the legendary playwrights and mathematicians that could be found in Athens. Instead, the focus was on physical and martial education, stealth, pain endurance, and loyalty to Sparta.

The regime was designed to turn the boys into the toughest of men, inured to the hardships of sustained military campaigns. They were deliberately underfed so they would be forced to steal food. Stealing was not a crime in itself, but getting caught was, and punishments were severe. The Greek historian Plutarch tells of a boy who had hidden a stolen fox under his cloak: he "suffered the animal to tear out his bowels with its teeth and claws, and died rather than have his theft detected."

The Spartans' famous loyalty and desire to protect the privileges of freedom did not extend to their relationships with other Greeks or the vast ranks of the helots, their slaves, on which their economy was based. Here their mercilessness and ingrained capacity for deception would come to the fore. They were happy to steal lands from other states by any means possible, while, according to the Greek historian Myron of Priene, every person enslaved by the Spartans would "receive a stipulated number of beatings every year regardless of any wrongdoing, so that they would never forget they were slaves."

In military terms, the other city-states of Ancient Greece in the fifth century BC were disorganized. There was very little systematic training of soldiers in readiness for war, but in Sparta it was the be all and end all. As Plutarch wrote in *The Life of Lycurgus*, "they were the only men in the world for whom war brought a respite in the training for war." Any male who failed military school could not even become a full citizen.

Opposite and above: Helmets covered the entire head except for the eyes, mouth, and chin

Sparta was not a large, well-populated region, so there were only 5,000 Spartiates at any one time. The very best of them formed the Spartan king Leonides' personal bodyguard, and it was this elite band of 300 men who faced the Persian multitudes at Thermopylae, which means "Hot Gates."

The Spartiates wore their hair long as a sign of their citizenry and democratic freedom, but their helmets were usually unadorned by plumes. Along with their red cloaks and sculpted breastplates, they carried a large round shield ornamented with a chevron, an inverted "V", the symbol of Sparta. They fought in phalanx formation—a block of soldiers usually at least eight rows deep—with their shields overlapping to form a wall of bronze. Protruding from this wall were their "dorys"—long spears that

Above: Statue of King Leonidas at Thermopylae, where he led his men to a glorious defeat

were held at shoulder height so they could stab over the top of the enemy's shields.

For even closer combat, especially when opposing phalanxes collided, the Spartiates would use their secondary weapon, the *xiphos*, a short sword. This was one of the Spartans' tactical secrets. The Spartan sword was considerably shorter than those of other Greek soldiers so that it could be wielded in very close combat to thrust into an unprotected throat or groin. When one Athenian soldier remarked that a Spartan's sword was short, he replied, "It's long enough to reach your heart." Some Spartans preferred a short curved sword, a *kopis*, which was better for slashing and causing carnage at close quarters. Failing that, the Spartans would resort to pankration, a martial art combining wrestling and boxing, at which they excelled like no other people.

The traditional phalanx formation did have a faultline: once the first line of defense was broken, a rupture could be driven through the entire phalanx, with those behind the front line often fleeing in chaos, abandoning their heavy shields. Consequently Spartans were trained never to dishonor themselves by breaking away from the line of battle, even in the face of certain death. To drop one's shield was regarded as dishonorable—a disgrace to Sparta. The shields were used as stretchers to carry the dead and injured from the battlefield. The Roman writer Plurarch recorded a famous instruction that Spartan women would give their menfolk before they went into battle: "Either return with your shield, or on it." The 300 at Thermopylae took those words to heart.

In 480 BC, the vast Persian Empire was threatening the city-states of Greece with an enormous, well-trained army. The Greek states were unprepared for their rapid onslaught, and so King Leonidas attempted to hold the Persians back at the mountain pass of Thermopylae with his personal bodyguard. It was tactical genius to diminish the advantage of the enemy by making the Persians fight in a narrow pass where they couldn't bring the full force of their army to bear. Ultimately, it was also suicidal.

To begin with the 300 were aided by a few thousand additional Greek soldiers from other city-states, but they retreated when the end became inevitable. In the final throes of the battle, only the Spartan 300 stood in the way of 150,000 Persians.

According to the Greek historian Herodotus, prior to the engagement a Persian envoy threatened the Spartans with the words, "Our arrows will darken the sky." The simple Spartan response was, "So we will fight in the shade." True to their word, after a failed light infantry attack, the Persians sent in wave after wave of cane arrows, which were repelled by the Spartan phalanxes raising their shields above their heads to form a cover. The phalanx formation was the perfect system for the defense of a tight mountain pass against far superior numbers. They were even able to fend off Persian cavalry charges.

DEATH OF THE PHALANX

THE PHALANX PRE-DATED the Spartans, but no previous force had been so well-drilled and effective in its execution. The formation of blocks of highly disciplined soldiers with overlapping shields, fighting as one unit, was the secret to their success on the battlefield and allowed Sparta to become an important political force. However, at the Battle of Sphacteria in 425 BC, Demosthenes, an Athenian general, worked out how to cripple the phalanx formation. Like later guerrilla warriors, he refused to engage the superior Spartans in open battle. He bombarded them with missiles from all sides; then when the Spartans repeatedly attempted to engage them in a full-on assault, his troops simply gave ground and then attacked them as they withdrew. Frustrated, weakened, and exhausted, the Spartans surrendered—for the first time in history. Then in 371 BC, at the Battle of Leuctra, the Spartans were defeated in open battle by the Thebans, who stacked their left wing and staggered their attack at a diagonal angle against the straight line of Spartan phalanxes. The Spartans were outmaneuvered and lost. The defeat led to Sparta becoming a second-rate power.

By then the Persian king, Xerxes, had realized that he would have to use his most elite troops to wipe out the irritating little band that stood in the way of his invasion of Greece. This elite force comprised 10,000 fearsome Achaemenid Persian infantry soldiers. Herodotus called them "those without deaths" or the Immortals, and recounts that "the king's Immortals ... advanced in full confidence of bringing the business to a swift and easy end." Their confidence was soon to be revealed as misplaced arrogance.

Below: Sculpture of a Spartan solider by Malcolm Lidbury

The longer spears of the Spartans meant that they were able to fight off the Immortals before they could get close enough to strike, while the Immortals' wicker shields were no match for Spartan weaponry. The Immortals proved to be mortal in the face of trained Spartan killers.

And yet the Spartans were undone. The 300 would all be slaughtered—because of the treachery and lies of a fellow Greek, Ephialtes. Contrary to the film *300*, he was not a resentful, deformed Spartan who had been spirited away into exile as a baby before he could be inspected by the Gerousia and left to die. Ephialtes was merely a local Greek from Trachis, just to the west of the Hot Gates, who felt no loyalty to the Spartans and was in search of a reward. Aware of the position that the Spartans had taken up at Thermopylae, he informed the Persians about a secret path that twisted through the mountainous terrain to join the road south of Thermopylae, behind the Spartan forces. Xerxes seized his chance.

Now they were being attacked from front and rear, the dwindling Spartan force could no longer hold out against the massive Persian army. Surrender was not an option. Every one of them had been trained to fight to the death for the glory of Sparta, and that's exactly what they did, killing thousands of Persians before they fell, one by one.

Dead on the battlefield, the elite 300 could not seek revenge, but justice was meted out in time. A bounty was put on the head of the treacherous Ephialtes, and he had to flee without collecting his reward from the Persians. According to Herodotus, he was killed by a fellow Greek from Trachis about a decade later.

The Spartans may have lost their most famous battle but had achieved their aim. They had held up the huge Persian force long enough for the combined Greek armies to prepare for the invasion. Instead of sweeping through Greece, Xerxes found himself entrenched in a long, difficult war. In 479 BC, the Spartans took their revenge and played a pivotal role in the defeat of the Persians at Plataea. The city-states of Greece had mustered around 100,000 men to fight the Persians, but only 5,000 were Spartiates.

Below: Ancient Greek pottery depicting a charioteer and horses

The Spartan commanders were once again brave in the face of impossible odds. They refused to retreat at times when the best strategic option was to withdraw. But it was typical Spartan determination—the ingrained desire to win—that led the Greeks to victory. The Spartiates formed the vanguard of an assault that broke the Persian line. The Persians were no match for them in close combat, and the Spartiates drove right through them and slew the Persian commander. The Persian invasion of Greece effectively ended on that day.

The Greeks may have fought together to evict the Persians, but the city-states would battle each other for decades in the Peloponnesian War. Sparta was able to become a dominant force in the region solely because of its martial elitism. However, other Greeks had their own skills, including education and invention. They learned everything they could about the

Right: Persian Immortals pictured at the Ishtar Gate of Ancient Babylon

Spartan military organization and adapted it to their own ends. They steadily began to create strategies to defy the Spartan military tactics.

Over the course of the next century, Sparta diminished as both a powerful city-state and an elite military force. Elite forces have to adapt to terrain and continually develop technological, tactical, and strategic methods. The other city-states copied Spartan military discipline and learned how to train a modern fighting force, but they also worked out how to utilize a mixture of light and heavy infantry in combination with a high level of maneuverability.

Meanwhile, the Spartan system was preserved in aspic. The Spartans persisted with their outmoded phalanx formation and their do-or-die psychological approach to battle. In the end, by dint of experience, their opponents knew exactly what they were going to do: there were no more secrets, no strategic surprises. The Spartiate hoplites, and thus the whole of Sparta, became a spent force, already fading from history by the 4th century BC.

Above: Leonidas at Thermopylae by Jacques-Louis David (1814)

Sacred Band of Thebes

The 150 pairs of male lovers who defeated the military might of Sparta in Ancient Greece

THE 300 WARRIORS stood tall and brave on the battlefield, fighting to the very last man while their fellow Greeks fled from the terrifying enemy. Yet they were not the legendary 300 of Sparta. They were the Sacred Band of Thebes, an elite unit who had proven themselves to be just as ruthless, disciplined and suicidally brave as their Spartan counterparts.

Prior to their last, fatal mission in 338 BC, the 300 soldiers of the Sacred Band helped to defeat Sparta and turn the city-state of Thebes into a major force in Ancient Greece. Camaraderie in elite forces is not unusual, but the level of devotion the Sacred Band had to each other was exceptional: they were all male lovers.

The exact date that the Sacred Band of Thebes was created cannot be pinpointed, but the unit emerged soon after the liberation of the Theban citadel of Cadmea from Sparta in 379 BC. Thebes had long been an enemy of the other great powers in Greece. It had even allied with the

FACT FILE

REGION: Ancient Greece
ERA: c.378–338 BC
KEY ENCOUNTERS: Battle of Tegyra 375 BC; Battle of Leuctra 371 BC; Battle of Chaeronea 338 BC
TACTICS AND TECHNIQUES: Used as shock unit in innovative left-sided attack against phalanx formations
WEAPONRY: Shield, long spear, short sword
LEGACY: Helped to defeat Sparta and turn Thebes into a dominant power

Persians during their attempted invasion of Greece in 480 BC, and fought alongside them at the Battle of Plataea, where the Spartans and Athenians proved victorious. After Sparta's victory in the Peloponnesian War, Thebes spearheaded the resistance to Spartan dominance, but Sparta captured its citadel in 382 BC.

Like the Athenians, the Thebans learned from the superior tactics and strategies of their Spartan oppressors. Gorgidas, a Theban politician, knew that a unified fighting spirit was essential to a military unit, so he created 150 pairs of male lovers to ensure that their commitment to each other was

Below: Depiction of fighting hoplites on pottery housed in the Athens Museum

absolute. Each couple was formed of an older, experienced soldier and a younger recruit. Homosexuality was frowned upon by some sections of Greek society, but it remained widely practiced even amongst married men. Trained recruits became full soldiers at around the age of 20 and served the Band for 10 years.

The soldiers of the Sacred Band of Thebes were equipped just like other hoplites in the armies of the Greek city-states: a large, round shield made of oak with a bronze outer layer, a bronze breastplate, a plumed helmet, a spear and a sword. However, Thebes had never had a fighting force like the Sacred Band. They were highly trained in combat skills, wrestling, and horsemanship. The Greek historian Plutarch claimed they were originally divided amongst the infantry in order to add an elite, drilled, highly skilled, and fearsome element, but they found fame fighting as a single unit under the command of Pelopidas during the Battle of Tegyra in 375 BC.

Above: The Lion of Chaeronea, the tomb for the 254 soldiers of the Sacred Band of Thebes who died in the Battle of Chaeronea in 338 BC

Opposite: A funerary stele (a commemorative stone) featuring a relief carving of a hoplite, *c.*400 BC

They were a secret weapon, acting as an elite shock force that would specifically engage the enemy's best troops on the frontline and kill their commanders, thereby immediately weakening and disrupting the entire opposition army.

Prior to the Battle of Tegyra, the Sacred Band were returning from a sortie into enemy territory when their route back to Thebes was blocked by a Spartan force. Even though the band of 300 and a small cavalry unit were facing an army at least twice their size, Pelopidas decided on a brave and perhaps foolish frontal assault. The copycats were taking on the old masters.

The band of lovers proved equal to the task and cut down the Spartan commanders, whose forces parted to allow them to continue on their way without further bloodshed. However, the Theban bloodlust was not sated, and they continued to scythe their way through the Spartan divisions until they were decimated, with the survivors fleeing for their lives.

It was a minor victory in numerical terms, but it was the first time that anyone had witnessed the Spartans fleeing in terror. The Spartan army was no longer seen as invincible, and the Thebans had proved that they were just as skilled and courageous as that almost mystical elite force. Plutarch wrote of the significance of the battle, adding, perhaps bizarrely, that the Sacred Band's shame over their own homosexuality had been a contributing factor: "For in all the great wars there had ever been against the Greeks or barbarians, the Spartans were never before beaten by a smaller company than their own ... [W]here the youth are ashamed of baseness, and ready to venture in a good cause, where they fly in disgrace more than danger, there, wherever it be, are found the bravest and most formidable opponents."

Below: An idealized hoplite on a grave relief

The Sacred Band of Thebes' proudest moment was still to come. In the Battle of Leuctra in 371 BC, they were set against the full might of the Spartan army. Pelopidas was so sure of the ability of the Sacred Band that he pitted them against the elite section of the Spartan forces.

The armies of the warring Greek city-states would usually fight in exactly the same formation. The force would be divided up into equally sized phalanxes, with the best forces placed on the right wing. The elite forces, hopefully, would push back the weaker phalanxes positioned on the enemy's left flank and force their way inwards towards the heart of the enemy formation, wreaking havoc. The only problem was that the Spartan elite on the right wing was far superior to any other force in open battle, and would inevitably win.

In a bold maneuver Pelopidas and his general, Epaminondas, put the Sacred Band on the left-wing, directly against the Spartan elite, supported by an unusually deep phalanx of 50 rows. The strategy was risky. If the specialized unit failed, the whole Theban force would soon be wiped out. Meanwhile, rather than meet the rest of the Spartan phalanxes face to face, Epaminondas sent the remainder of his outnumbered forces into battle at an angle, which disrupted the straight-set Spartan formation.

Pelopidas counted on the Sacred Band's devotion for one another in the face of death—along with their high level of specialist military training. His faith was rewarded. Incredibly, the Sacred Band not only matched the Spartan elite warriors, they pushed right through them and killed their king, Cleombrotus. The Spartiates, who had never before been beaten in open battle, were annihilated. A tremor of shock ran through the ancient world. Sparta, as both a political and military force, was crippled.

As a direct result of the valor of the small Sacred Band of Thebes, their city-state became the dominant power in the whole of Greece. Following the Battle of Leuctra, Thebes freed a huge multitude of slaves in Sparta. The slave system was the heart of the Spartan economy and had enabled it to use its entire male citizenry as a permanent army—without its slaves, Sparta evaporated as a notable military force.

The Sacred Band continued to play a part in Theban successes, but in 338 BC they faced their own annihilation. A new leader had emerged in

SACRED BANDS

THE SACRED BAND of Thebes were neither priests nor particularly holy. Instead, according to the historian Plutarch, they took the name "Sacred Band" simply because the 150 pairs of male partners shared vows of love at the shrine of Iolaus, the nephew and lover of Hercules. The appellation "Sacred Band" was taken up by other military units throughout history, again without any religious significance: it indicated that, like the Thebans, they were devout in the pursuit of their cause. The Sacred Band of Carthage was a phalanx of 2,000 spearmen in the 4th century BC, notorious only for being wiped out on two occasions before being disbanded. Later Sacred Bands include a battalion formed in 1821 during the Greek War of Independence, which was destroyed within a year, and a Greek unit formed in World War II. The latter fought valiantly in 1942–5 and became the model for the modern-day Greek special forces.

Above: The Death of Epaminondas by Isaac Walraven (1726), showing the great Theban military strategist

Macedonia: Philip II, father of Alexander the Great, was to prove a new type of military and tactical genius, and he was intent on taking control of Greece.

The Thebans were losing power not just in Greece, but in their own central region. They had defeated a combined force of Spartans and Athenians in 362 BC, but their key military strategist, Epaminondas, died in the fighting. Without him, Thebes could no longer even control its troublesome neighbor, the state of Phocis. The Thebans made the mistake of asking the increasingly powerful and politically astute Philip of Macedon for assistance. He duly took control of Phocis, and Thebes found itself with a far more dangerous neighbor.

Thebes entered an alliance with Athens in order to defeat Philip. Their combined armies of 30,000 soldiers faced the Macedonian king and his equally sized force at Chaeronea in 338 BC. It was to prove to be the only battle that the Sacred Band of Thebes would lose, and also their last.

The Greek historian Diodorus wrote that the battle "was hotly contested for a long time and many fell on both sides, so that for a while the struggle permitted hopes of victory to both." However, the Macedonians gained the upper hand, partly because Philip's son, Alexander, who would become the greatest military commander the ancient world had ever known, was "set on showing his father his prowess."

Philip outmaneuvered the inexperienced Athenians by feigning a retreat on the right wing, drawing them into a disorganized push forward, and performing a wheeling stratagem. This allowed Alexander, leading the Macedonian left wing, to punch a hole through the Theban right, where the elite Sacred Band of Thebes were stationed. It was a rout.

Like the Spartan 300, the Theban 300 gave up their lives in a valorous but suicidal mission. The main Theban and Athenian contingents fled in the face of slaughter, but the Sacred Band held their ground in an attempt to protect the retreat of their fellow soldiers. Not one of them ran and, completely surrounded, each man fought to the death.

Below: Alexander the Great, the greatest military leader of the ancient world

In victory, Philip was magnanimous about the formerly invincible band of lovers. According to Plutarch, who grew up in Chaeronea, when Philip saw the heaped bodies of the 300 dead lovers, he cried and said, "As for anyone who thinks these men did or suffered anything disgraceful, may they perish miserably." A stone lion was erected to mark the place where the unit fell. Recently, excavations have revealed the bones of 254 soldiers underneath the monument: the remains of the Sacred Band of Thebes.

The Battle of Chaeronea was one the most significant conflicts in ancient history. Thebes, and Athens soon surrendered and the warring city-states were collectively diminished to the role of enforced allies of a greater power: Macedonia. After the assassination of Philip, the Thebans revolted, but Alexander was not as merciful as his father. He removed the problem of Thebes entirely by destroying the city and selling its citizens into slavery.

Praetorian Guard

The elite unit which protected—and sometimes killed—Roman emperors in a time rife with plots and assassinations

ON THE IDES of March, 44 BC, the seemingly all-powerful Julius Caesar was surrounded by senators, including his apparent friends and allies, and repeatedly stabbed until his body lay lifeless. In an era of intrigue, secrets, lies, and assassinations, his nephew Octavian wanted to ensure that he would never befall his uncle's fate.

As soon as Octavian became Augustus Caesar, Emperor of Rome, he announced the creation of the Praetorian Guard, his personal, elite bodyguard. Augustus wanted a permanent, fear-inducing unit whose raison d'être was to defend the emperor with utmost loyalty. The emperors of Rome were the most powerful men in the world for centuries to come, but often it was the Praetorian Guard who decided their fate. They were both the Empire's king-makers and its assassins. Augustus had unwittingly left the fate of Rome in the hands of an elite who would soon become the champions of murderous intrigue, secrets, and lies. Throughout history, their name would become a slur directed at military elites such as the Ottoman Janissaries, who held their rulers to ransom for the sake of their own wealth and power.

FACT FILE

REGION: Ancient Rome
ERA: 27 BC–AD 312
KEY ENCOUNTERS: First Battle of Bedriacum AD 69; Dismissed with dishonor AD 193; Battle of the Milvian Bridge AD 312
TACTICS AND TECHNIQUES: Fearsome city-based unit who controlled Rome with the threat of force and assassinated emperors
WEAPONRY: Javelin, sword and shield
LEGACY: Changed the history of the Roman Empire by supporting or murdering imperial rivals

Above: Statue of Augustus Caesar, Capri

The Praetorian Guard was created by Augustus at the birth of the Roman Empire in 27 BC, but was predated by the Praetoria Cohors, a specialist unit that had guarded generals on the battlefield during the old Roman Republic.

The Praetorian Guard was originally made up of nine cohorts, each comprised of 500 men, and later expanded to ten larger cohorts. They were immediately regarded as the most important force in the entire Roman army; the soldiers were paid more and served a shorter term, so they were able to choose from the very best recruits. Only full Roman citizens could join; foreigners, slaves, and even freemen who had won the right to citizenry would not be trusted with the life of the emperor. The emperor himself was their commander, aided by a hierarchy led by a Praetorian prefect, tribunes, and centurions.

As well as being an elite personal bodyguard, the Praetorians were also engaged in many other tasks linked to the preservation of the political status quo in Rome, including maintaining the public order of the city and keeping a watchful eye on any threats to the state. Consequently, they used various intelligence techniques, and had a network of informers and spies. They were the only military force allowed to bear arms within the gates of Rome, which meant that they often held the fate of the empire in their hands. On many occasions they were happy to use their unique position to the utmost effect.

Below: Augustus established a household guard for his own protection as soon as he became emperor in 27 BC

The uniform and weaponry of the Praetorian Guards were little different from those of a typical legionnaire. They wore a white tunic cut to above the knee, a cloak, a helmet, and armor, and were armed with a javelin, sword, and shield. The shield initially made the Praetorian stand out as it was oval rather than rectangular, but the standard rectangular shield was adopted in the 2nd century. However, the shields often continued to bear the feared image of a scorpion, a sign to a would-be attacker that they were facing the imperial elite. Their standard-bearers were also distinguished by lion pelts covering their helmets.

After the death of Augustus, his successor Tiberius faced mutiny amongst the legions, which the highly trained Praetorians helped to quell under the command of Tiberius' nephew and adopted son, Germanicus. One of the greatest generals in the early Roman Empire, Germanicus thought highly of the skills and discipline of the Guard and used several divisions in his successful conquest of Germania.

The Guards' sense of unity and uniqueness was furthered in AD 23 when they moved to the Castra Praetoria, a purpose-built, fortified barracks on the edge of Rome. Emperor Tiberius' powerful Praetorian prefect Sejanus was behind the decision, as the Roman historian Tacitus explained, increasing "the influence of the prefecture by gathering into a single camp the cohorts scattered across the city ... there would be a rise in their own confidence and the dread of everyone else."

When Sejanus became too powerful, Tiberius had him executed. The city was in political turmoil, and there was a moment at which the Praetorian Guard, some of whom took the opportunity to commence looting, could have turned against their emperor. They chose restraint in return for an imperial "donation," but by that time there was no doubt that the Guard was a powder keg that could be ignited to change the fortunes of the Empire.

AD 41 would reveal just how willing the Praetorian Guard was to embroil itself in the politics of Rome. The mentally unstable Emperor Caligula had become involved in scandals and had even announced his own divinity, but his biggest mistake was to repeatedly mock a Praetorian centurion, Cassius Chaerea. According to the historian Suetonius, whenever Cassius had to kiss the emperor's ring, Caligula would "hold out his hand to kiss,

Below: Augustus (right), who founded the Praetorian Guard, and Constantine, who dismantled it 300 years later

Above: Proclaiming Claudius Emperor by Sir Lawrence Alma-Tadema (1867) shows the Praetorian Guards as the king-makers of the empire

forming and moving it in an obscene fashion," and made him use profane watchwords such as "*priapus*" (erection). A skilled soldier who had proved himself on the battlefield and suffered injury in the cause of Rome, Cassius Chaerea was not a man to be trifled with and, politically, he abhorred the debasement of the office of emperor.

Consequently it was Cassius Chaerea who led a conspiracy of Praetorian guards and pro-republican senators to assassinate Caligula. It seems that he relished the act. The historian Cassius Dio describes the scene: "The followers of Chaerea could endure it no longer ... the conspirators wounded [Caligula], then intercepted him in a narrow passage and killed him. When he fell to the ground none of those present would keep his hands off him but they all savagely stabbed the lifeless corpse again and again. Some chewed pieces of his flesh."

The senators and Cassius Chaerea wanted to announce the return of the democratic Roman republic. But for the Praetorian Guard, the Roman Empire could have ended at that moment, and the future of Europe, the Middle East, and North Africa would have been very different. For the Guard did not share Cassius' republican ideals and had its own agenda. Many of the guards did not want to give up the privileged imperial status they would have lost in a reconstituted republic, so they smuggled Claudius, Caligula's supposedly imbecilic uncle and heir, out of the city to the Castra Praetoria.

With Praetorian support, Claudius was made emperor—the Senate did not dare to oppose the Guard and the republican movement was broken. The importance of the Praetorian Guard to the future of the Empire was underlined when Claudius minted his first coin. On one side of the coin was his own portrait; on the other was an image of the Castra Praetoria, complete with a Praetorian standard-bearer.

It was not long until the Praetorian Guard again played a pivotal role in the fortunes of the emperors. In AD 68, when Emperor Nero was facing mounting opposition from a rival, Galba, the Praetorian prefect refused to support him. Nero knew that without the Guard's protection the writing was on the wall, and he chose death. Galba became emperor but he failed to pay a promised donation to the Guards. As a result, they assassinated him in AD 69 and transferred their allegiance to Otho, who was willing to pay the donation and also allowed them to appoint their own prefect.

ROMAN BODYGUARDS

AS THE CONTINUAL machinations of the Praetorian Guards meant that they could not be trusted, some emperors turned to other elite units to preserve their safety. Both Caligula and Nero preferred German bodyguards for close personal protection. At the end of the 3rd century, Diocletian stripped the Praetorians of their role as bodyguards and instead used two units from Illyria in the Balkans. Constantine then created the elite *scholae* as an imperial force, which continued to guard Byzantine emperors until the 11th century. They were highly trained cavalry originally made up of Frank, Alaman and Goth barbarian warriors. He preferred to put his faith in a trained barbarian soldier than a disloyal Roman guardsman with a predilection for forced "donations" and political games.

Except for the campaign in Germany, the role of the Praetorian Guard had been centered on Rome, and the guards usually only left the city to protect the emperor on his travels. However, in AD 69 they showed that they were willing to take to the battlefield in order to influence the fate of the Empire. At the First Battle of Bedriacum, the guards fought in open warfare for the first time in decades. They were endeavoring to protect Emperor Otho against his rival, Vitellius. They may have been a feared elite force within the walls of Rome, but they were taunted by Vitellius' experienced campaigning forces for being bloated by their life of excess and leisure in the capital. Otho lost the battle and committed suicide, and the guards had to adjust to life under a new emperor who despised them.

Below: Relief of a Roman legionary

Vitellius deliberately weakened the Guard's elite hardcore by dismissing its senior guards and establishing additional cohorts with fresh recruits. Naturally, when the newcomer Vespasian mounted a campaign against Vitellius, he could rely on the disgruntled Guard for support; he knew just how powerful they were. After ousting Vitellius, Vespasian restored the Guard to its former nine cohorts, but he made his son, Titus, the Praetorian prefect to ensure that he would not be the next emperor to feel the cut of their cold steel.

Under Emperor Domitian, who came to power in AD 81, the Praetorians become more active in military campaigns. The guardsmen were fond of Domitian, and consequently lynched his murderers in AD 97. In the 2nd century both Trajan, in his wars against Dacia, and Marcus Aurelius, in his battles against the German tribes, relied on their military skill. By this time, the original purpose of the Praetorian Guard had become diluted and most of the unit spent less time in Rome.

In the course of their history, early emperors had valued the elite skills of the Praetorian Guard as a personal protection unit, and later emperors admired their valor on the field of battle. Septimius Severus, on the other hand, dismissed the whole Guard with dishonor as soon as he came to power in AD 193, a year in which there were three emperors. The Guard had returned to their dishonorable ways, assassinating Emperor Pertinax early that year. Their power was such that they were then able to sell off control of the world's greatest empire to the highest bidder. Didius Julianus paid a huge sum for the privilege. However, he lasted only three months before he was killed.

Septimius blamed the Guard for the chaos and the debasement of the Empire. After the mass dismissal, recruits were no longer picked solely from Rome and the older, more historically loyal sectors of the Empire. Any legionnaire could join, and its cohorts, now ten of them, became subsumed into the main army. From that year onwards, the Praetorian Guard was no longer an elite unit.

Above: Roman marble relief with members of the Praetorian Guard

However, that did not put a stop to the Guard's role as a powerbroker in the fate of the Empire. They continued to take sides in the conflicts between imperial rivals and were involved in the murder of Caracalla in AD 217, who was replaced by their own prefect, Macrinus. After Macrinus was defeated in battle by Elagabalus, a Syrian who the Guards did not favor, they took revenge against the new emperor and his mother in bloodthirsty fashion. Cassius Dio reports that in AD 222, "their heads were cut off and their bodies, after being stripped naked, were first dragged all over the city." The co-emperors Balbinus and Pupienus were also given short shrift; they were murdered by the Praetorians just three months after coming to power in AD 238.

As it was no longer elite, emperors began to see the Praetorian Guard as merely a disruptive, potentially disloyal, and destabilizing force that would not ensure the emperor's safety while simultaneously draining the coffers. Emperor Diocletian reduced the unit's size at the end of the 3rd century and replaced it with foreign units as his personal protection team. After almost three centuries, the Guard had lost its place as a powerful force at the heart of the Empire. By the time Diocletian left office in 305, the soldiers were no longer a regular feature of palace life in Rome, and the large barracks at the Castra Praetoria housed only a small garrison.

The following year, the Praetorian Guard made a bold attempt to maintain its historical role as a powerbroker. It was a last throw of the dice. With its existence under threat, the guards supported the ill-fated Maxentius in his attempt to become emperor, despite the rest of the army favoring Constantine in what became a civil war. They fought for Maxentius against Constantine at the Battle of the Milvian Bridge in AD 312. When Maxentius drowned in the river Tiber as the battle raged around him, the future of the Praetorian Guard died with him.

The victorious Constantine disbanded the Guard, sent its soldiers to the far reaches of the Empire, and, in a highly symbolic act, destroyed the Castra Praetoria. The 300 year-old elite military unit, which had enjoyed more power and was more embroiled in a web of secrets and lies than any other military unit in world history, was finally no more.

Opposite: Head of a colossal statue of Constantine; the full statue would have been about 40 ft (12 m) high

Varangian Guard

The ax-wielding warriors whom the Byzantine emperors trusted more than their own army

"THE VARANGIANS FIGHT like madmen as if ablaze with wrath ... They do not spare themselves, they do not care about their wounds, and they despise their bodies." These are the words of the Byzantine monk Michael Psellus describing the mighty Varangian Guard, an elite mercenary unit, who made the enemies of the Byzantine Empire tremble with fear.

As well as its training, strategies, tactical deployment, and weaponry, the power of an elite lies in its ability to cause fear—the fear that these soldiers will do anything, way beyond normal human capacity, to win. The enemy is beaten before it even takes to the field. The Varangians had that power, partly because they were Viking warriors. It gave them mythical status.

In 988 Basil II, the Byzantine Emperor, needed additional troops to put down the rebellion of a local general, Bardas Phocas. Prince Vladimir of Kiev provided the perfect solution. In return for the hand in marriage of Basil's sister, he sent the Emperor 6,000 Varangians—the Slavic term for Vikings, derived from the Old Norse for "pledged companions," a reference to their fraternal loyalty in war.

The original Norse soldiers were of the same stock as the Viking warriors who had pillaged the shores of Europe and beyond for the preceding two centuries. Vladimir

FACT FILE

REGION: Byzantine Empire
ERA: 988–1204
KEY ENCOUNTERS: Battle of Chrysopolis 988; Battle of Beroia 1122; Sacking of Constantinople 1204
Tactics and techniques: Bodyguard unit also used as shock troops at the pivotal stage of battles
WEAPONRY: Two-handed ax, sword, spear
LEGACY: Supported the Byzantine empire for 200 years

had hired the Varangians while he was in Scandinavia preparing to mount an assault on his brother, Yaropolk, who had taken the important Russian city of Novgorod from him. Some of the Varangians had already settled in the Novgorod area in the 9th century, and he was familiar with their martial skills. The Varangians proved their worth, capturing both Novgorod and Kiev on behalf of Vladimir. However, the Russian ruler was more than happy to part with them as a gift. Fierce, warring, heavy-drinking, and supposedly obstreperous by nature, they had been useful in wartime, but Vladimir now sought to have a settled, peaceful realm, and he knew they could cause no end of trouble.

Above: The Bayeux Tapestry, showing ax-wielding housecarls (see page 43) facing a charge, 1066; Scandinavian and English warriors who had faced each other at Stamford Bridge later fought together in the Varangian Guard

Right: The Coronation of the Byzantine Emperor Basil II, who established the Varangian Guard in 988

Right: A Thracian woman kills a Varangian who tried to rape her; the assailant's more honorable fellow soldiers surrender his belongings to her

Pockets of Varangian mercenaries had already fought in the Byzantine region, gaining a good reputation, so Basil welcomed the gift. Almost as soon as they arrived en masse in the Byzantine Empire, he led them into the Battle of Chrysopolis on the Bosporus.

It was soon confirmed that he had been sent the most loyal and courageous mercenaries he had ever encountered. Phocas had hired his own mercenary force of Iberians, whom Psellus described as "the finest fighters ... in the flower of their youth." They were, however, no match for the Scandinavians, who were disciplined, aggressive, and merciless in battle.

As the Iberians discovered, the Varangian Guard had a unique capacity as a shock force fighting in the Scandinavian style. The secret to their fierce and courageous fighting lay in the frenzied, high-adrenalin trance they would work themselves into prior to battle. This would make them immune to pain (copious amounts of alcohol may also have helped). They then rushed into battle at speed, despite their heavy armor and the weight of their favorite weapon, the long, two-handed ax. This was wielded with such ferocity that carnage would ensue, often leading to the enemy fleeing the battlefield. As a result, they became known as the "ax-bearing barbarians," and like their Viking forebears, the "beserkers." As the ax required two hands, the Varangian warriors would dangle a sword from their right shoulder, switching weapons to swiftly dispatch their victims after they had been felled by the ax. They also used spears and were competent horsemen.

From the Battle of Chrysopolis until the beginning of the 14th century, they fought in every major campaign conducted by the Byzantine emperors. They were pivotal in maintaining a Byzantine foothold in Italy in the first half of the 11th century, routing the Lombards at the Battle of Cannae in 1018. However, they suffered the ignominy of being present at the Battle of Manzikert in 1071 when the Seljuk Turks crushed Byzantine forces, although they fought bravely to protect Emperor Romanos IV before he was captured.

Left: The Byzantine Emperor John II Komnenos, who commanded the Varangians at the successful Battle of Beroia, 1122

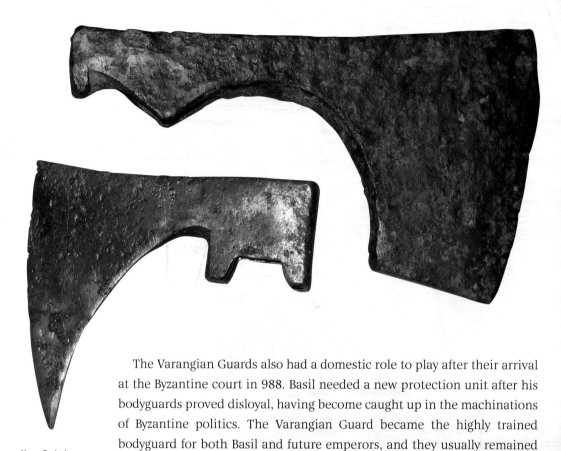

Above: Typical Varangian axheads

The Varangian Guards also had a domestic role to play after their arrival at the Byzantine court in 988. Basil needed a new protection unit after his bodyguards proved disloyal, having become caught up in the machinations of Byzantine politics. The Varangian Guard became the highly trained bodyguard for both Basil and future emperors, and they usually remained impervious to political jockeying and loyally obeyed the hand that fed them.

The Byzantine era was rife with conspiracies, revolts, and attempts to dethrone the emperor. There are claims that the Varangians were used as ruthless assassins within the court but little evidence to support this. But they were a menacing bodyguard, as Princess Anna Komnene described in her account of a plot against her father, Emperor Alexios I Komnenos (1056–1118), by a man named Solomon: "The soldiers who from of old were his appointed bodyguard came to the emperor's tent first, some wearing swords, others carrying spears or their heavy iron axes on their shoulders, and ranged themselves in the form of a crescent at a certain distance from his throne, embracing him, as it were; they were all under the sway of anger. [Solomon] looked fixedly ... at the barbarians ... brandishing their one-edged axes on their shoulders, and forthwith fell to trembling and revealed everything."

It was not only their fighting and bodyguard skills that made the Varangians legendary. They were the highest paid mercenaries in the Byzantine empire, and were given a significant share of war booty as well as imperial gifts. Consequently, over the years they were joined by more Viking blood: Norwegians, Danes, Icelanders, and Swedes travelled to the Byzantine capital of Constantinople in pursuit of wealth. Only the very best were allowed to join the Guard, and membership incurred a hefty fee. Nevertheless the military drain from Scandinavia was concerning: the Swedes even drafted a law forbidding anyone who stayed in the Byzantine Empire from inheriting property in their native land.

The most famous Varangian was Harald Sigurdsson, also known as Hardrada ("stern counsel"), who became the king of Norway in 1046. He served in the Varangian Guard from about 1034 and took part in Byzantine campaigns in Sicily, Bulgaria, and possibly the Holy Land. He is likely to have commanded a division in Bulgaria, but the Norsemen could not become generals, no matter what leadership qualities and tactical acumen they demonstrated, as this remained the privilege of Byzantine Greeks. However, the Varangians were responsible for their own discipline. They created laws to ensure that they remained a tight, highly trained brotherhood, and administered harsh penalties to anyone who stepped out of line.

VIKING HOUSECARLS

THE VARANGIAN GUARD was not the only elite Viking unit to form a royal bodyguard. The *húskarl* or housecarl—which literally means "house man" or manservant—had been a feature of Scandinavian life since at least the 9th century. They were armed freemen who were retainers in a king's or lord's personal household. Cnut, who became King of England in 1016, established a retinue of around 3,000 housecarls as his personal armed unit in the English court. They were a well-equipped, trained, professional standing army who were oath-bound to the king and followed a strict code of behavior. The housecarls were the mainstay of Harold Godwinson's defeated army at the Battle of Hastings in 1066, and fought to the very last man—even after the king had been slain.

The Guard had some level of respect within the Byzantine court—Harald held the court title of Spartharocandidatas—and they resided in decent quarters within the imperial palace. As explained in the 13th-century Icelandic collection of sagas, *Heimskringla*: "In Constantinople there are two suites of rooms in the palace occupied by the Imperial Guard, one above the other ... the Greek soldiers and Varangians disagreed about these rooms, and the matter was settled by drawing lots. [Harald] and the Varangians obtained the upper rooms, and from that time it has been the rule that these upper rooms have been occupied by Norsemen."

It was the huge rewards that Harald reaped as a Guard that enabled him to mount a successful challenge to the Norwegian throne. He later also attempted to invade England, but was defeated and killed at the Battle of Stamford Bridge in 1066. The English may have defeated the Norseman, but they were too weak to fend off William of Normandy later the same year.

In a peculiar circularity of history, the subsequent Norman occupation led many of England's finest warriors to seek their fortune as members of the Varangian Guard, fighting alongside the kinsmen of the Scandinavians they had repelled just months earlier. However, they were not peculiar bedfellows: the Anglo-Saxons and Scandinavians both came from fierce warrior stock and had a tradition of fighting to the death in the service of their masters.

By the time of the Battle of Beroia in 1122, one of the Varangians' greatest victories, there were probably more Englishmen in the Guard than Scandinavians. However, the tactics had not changed: the Varangians were still used as shock troops, entering the fray at a vital point in the battle, and frequently changing the

Below: John II Komnenos, whose Varangian Guards included many Englishmen after the Norman Conquest

course of the fighting to emerge victorious.

Emperor John II Komnenos launched a surprise attack on an army of Pecheneg nomads who had set up a circular laager—a fortification made up of wagons to form an improvised military camp—at Beroia (now called Stara Zagora in Bulgaria). The Byzantine assault failed, and they suffered heavy losses, which angered John, who had been wounded in the leg.

According to the sagas, his soldiers asked him to send in his "wine-bags"—the Varangians—which hints that the level of drinking in their ranks had not been diluted by the presence of Anglo-Saxons. John responded that he did not wish to waste his "jewels" in a battle that should already have been won, but the leading Varangian Thorir Helsing said he would willingly jump into the fire to please the Emperor. John relented. Headed by Thorir, the ax-wielding bezerkers smashed and hacked their way through the wagons, leaving the Pecheneg force vulnerable. A rout inevitably followed.

Above: John II Komnenos and the Virgin Mary holding the cross

The final chapter in the history of the Varangian Guard came in 1204. The Fourth Crusade had been mounted by Pope Innocent III and was originally meant to be sent to Egypt. However, its army of soldiers from France, Venice, and the Holy Roman Empire got diverted to Constantinople, seat of Byzantine Christianity, which was continually at odds with the Roman papacy.

The Varangian Guard, for once, proved itself to be neither valiant nor loyal. Initially, they had been amongst the fiercest protectors of the city, engaging in a terrifying, bloody battle with the Venetians. But then, with the siege of the ancient capital reaching a critical point, the imperial bodyguard refused to take any further part unless they were given a huge pay rise. When their demands were rejected, the Varangian Guard, the loyal, honorable, and fierce defendants of the Byzantine empire for more than 200 years, simply melted away or surrendered. Without them, Constantinople was sacked.

Hashishins

The warrior class of the Nizari Ismaili after whom all modern-day assassins are named

WHEN HE WOKE UP in the middle of the night, the great Saladin found a knife stuck into his pillow. He knew what it meant without even reading the accompanying note: he had been marked out for assassination by a select band of trained killers. The knife was no idle warning that death might be imminent: it was statement of fact. He knew that unless he created an alliance with the Nizari Ismaili, and soon, he would be laying his head on that pillow for the final time.

Saladin, the founder of the Ayyubid dynasty in the Middle East, was far from alone in fearing this particular band of assassins in the 11th to the 13th centuries. Many Sunni leaders, politicians, and scholars, as well as Christian Crusaders, would have their lives taken by the assassins of the Nizari Ismaili, a class of Shia Muslims who were surrounded by religious enemies, but had found a cunning way to fight back.

The assassins become known as the "Hashishins" because they allegedly consumed hashish before committing their murders, and that name evolved into the modern-day word "assassin," which since the 13th century has been applied to a person who murders for political or religious reasons. The root of the word is

FACT FILE

REGION: Iran and Syria
ERA: 11th to 14th century
KEY ENCOUNTERS: Assassination of Nizam al-Mulk 1092; Assassination of Sir Conrad de Montferrat 1192; Destruction of Alamut 1256
TACTICS AND TECHNIQUES: Elite covert unit trained in stealth, combat and assassination
WEAPONRY: Dagger
LEGACY: Enabled the establishment of the Nizari Ismaili, which now has 15 million followers

disputed, as is the consumption of hashish, but to some the tale that the Nizari assassins were hashish-eaters finds some credibility in the demeanor of the killers. After the murder, the Hashishin did not run away, but calmly stood by the victim until the body was discovered, and then allowed themselves to be sacrificed for their cause. This added to the assassins' reputation for fearlessness, and ensured that everyone knew exactly who was responsible for the murder.

Consequently the assassins were also known by the more honorable title of the Fedayeen, "the men who accept death." Various groups referring to themselves as Fedayeen have acted as militants, guerilla, and religious assassins in the history of the Middle East. However, "Hashishin," believed to have been first used in 1122 by a Mustaali Ismaili caliph, has continued to

Below: A group of assassins is instructed by the Old Man of the Mountain (Hassan-i Sabbah) in a Persian miniature

Above: A Persian miniature of the Moghul Khulug Khan's siege of Alamut, the fortress where Hassan-i Sabbah established his assassin elite

be used as a pejorative term by followers of other Muslim paths and historians from the West.

The Nizari Ismaili are at odds with the Sunni branch of Islam because they dispute the succession of the Prophet Muhammad. Like most Shia Muslims, they believe that Muhammad's relative Ali was nominated to be the Imam - the spiritual leader of Islam. The Nizari Ismaili believe that the Imamate has descended through the male line until the present day. These important distinctions continue to cause a rift in Islam throughout the world to this day, and they lie at the heart of numerous bitter wars, assassinations, and religious attacks.

The founder of the Nizari path of Islam and instigator of the assassin elite was Hassan-i Sabbah. Towards the end of the 11th century, the leader of the Ismaili in Persia created a Shia stronghold in the Alborz mountains, a northern area surrounded by Sunni Muslims. Hassan managed to convert the local community around the fortress of Alamut to the Ismaili path, and in 1090 gained control of the fortress. Hassan-i Sabbah was a scholar and Alamut became a centre of intellectual learning, with great libraries and serene gardens. It is said that Hassan, who knew the Qur'an by heart, left his personal quarters only twice in 35 years, and then only to go up to the roof of the fortress. His influence, though, was felt far and wide, not least in the form of the secret order of assassins he sent out from the fortress walls.

The assassins' most famous victim was Nizam al-Mulk, the vizier of Malik Shah I, the Sunni ruler of the Great Seljuk Empire. The Seljuks controlled a vast region stretching from the Persian Gulf to China, and Nizam al-Mulk was the Empire's administrative and military mastermind. Aware of Hassan-i Sabbah's growing influence even before his takeover of Alamut fortress, Nizam had already sent a force to the Alborz mountains to find and kill him. The mission failed. In October 1092, Hassan struck back. While Nizam was being carried on his litter on the road to Baghdad, he was approached by a man dressed in the typical attire of a Sufi dervish. He was actually a member of the Hashishins in disguise. The assassin stabbed him to death with a dagger.

Soon the Nizari Ismaili were able to extend their influence in Persia and Syria, setting up further strongholds. They were always outnumbered by their enemies, so instead of facing opponents in open battle, they ensured their fortresses were well fortified while attacking their opponents in the form of the selective elimination of their political and religious leaders. Civilians, though, were never targeted for assassination.

The assassins largely came from the Lasiq or "Adherent" class of Nizari Ismaili followers. It is thought that they were picked out as strong and agile young men. They were then trained in stealth, strategy, martial arts, knife

Left: Mamluk hammam at the Ismaili Castle (also known as the Hashishins' or Assassins' Castle), Masyaf, Syria; the assassins were active in the region until the 14th century

Above: Two statues bring together Saladin (right), the great Sultan of Egypt and Syria who was sent a personal threat by the Nizari assassins, and his bitter rival, Richard the Lionheart

combat, and equestrianism, as well as disguise. The dagger, sometimes dipped in poison, was their preferred weapon. They were also taught the value of patience and learnt covert skills so they could meld into their surroundings, having sometimes even learnt the local language to aid their assimilation.

The students, who devoutly followed a strict code of conduct, probably went through stages of initiation before being sent on an assassination mission, although their ideological training was just as important. They were religious warriors, taking part in *jihad* to remove the enemies of their faith. Marco Polo, the explorer, was partly responsible for the legend of hashish consumption. He wrote that the "Old Man of the Mountain"—supposedly Hassan-i Sabbah, though he had been dead for over a century at the time of writing—was drugging his disciples with hashish so they would selflessly follow his orders, while also promising them a return trip to paradise. In truth, the assassins were probably intoxicated by nothing more than religious fervor.

The assassins did not always kill their targets, but used their burgeoning notoriety in a form of psychological warfare, especially when dealing with the powerful sultans. After Ahmad Sanjar became Sultan of the Seljuk Empire in 1118, Hassan-i Sabbah sent him two messages: the first was a dagger stuck into the ground alongside his bed; the second was a note wishing the sultan well, implying that it had been good fortune that the dagger had been stuck in the ground and not his chest. The Seljuks stopped harassing the Nizari for decades afterwards.

Saladin, the Sultan of Egypt and Syria and widely known for his military prowess, waged a campaign against the Nizari Ismaili in 1176. Saladin was so wary of assassination that he supposedly surrounded his campaign tent with cinders so that he could hear the approach of even the stealthiest Fedayeen. Nevertheless, one night he awoke to see an intruder quietly leaving his tent and found an assassin's warning note pinned to his pillow with a dagger. Consequently he ceased his campaign and formed an alliance with the Nizari Ismaili against the Crusaders. As a result of this conciliatory move, his life was spared.

FEDAYEEN

THE "HASHISHINS" OR assassins of the Nizari Ismaili were the original fedayeen, which can mean "the martyrs," "the men who accept death," "the redeemers" or "the men who sacrifice." They established a tradition of armed militant groups in the Middle East who were willing to both take life and be killed for their religious beliefs. They are usually secret operators acting outside government control and state military influence. The Palestinian fedayeen predated the Palestinian Liberation Organization, emerging after the Arab-Israeli War of 1948 to conduct missions in Israeli territory from their bases in the West Bank and Gaza Strip. Fedayeen were also trained to fight and kill the British in Egypt in the 1940s, in the run up to the Suez Crisis. Various Iranian groups used the title "fedayeen" in the 20th century, including defenders of Islam and Sharia law, as well as a leftist group which conducted a series of political assassinations in a campaign against the Shah.

Several Crusaders are believed to have been assassinated by the Nizari Ismaili; the most notable was Sir Conrad de Montferrat, a victim of the assassins' penchant for disguise. A leading knight of the Third Crusade, he was elected King of Jerusalem in April 1192. Just a few days later, before he was even crowned, Sir Conrad was returning to his lodgings in the fortress of Tyre, accompanied by his personal bodyguard. As he walked through a courtyard, two assassins dressed as Christian monks approached and stabbed him in the side and back. The Crusader died from his wounds. One assassin was killed by the bodyguards, while the other was captured.

Under torture the surviving assassin claimed that they had been hired by Richard the Lionheart, King of England, who had opposed Conrad's appointment. This supposed confession may have been an act of deflection, as Conrad certainly had many other enemies, not least amongst Muslims, and some historians point the finger of blame at Saladin. Ibn al-Athir, the contemporary Islamic historian, wrote of the murder: "the greatest devil of all the Franks, Conrad de Montferrat—God damn him!—was killed."

The assassins ceased to be a military influence in Persia in the middle of the 13th century when the Mongols destroyed many of their fortresses, including Alamut in 1256. Despite their demise in Persia, the assassins of the Nizari Ismaili are thought to have undertaken the attempted assassination of Prince Edward Longshanks, the future King Edward I of England, in June 1272. Edward took part in the Ninth Crusade and was disgusted that the West's nominal king of Jerusalem, Hugh III of Cyrus, had agreed a truce with the Mamluks and their force of Muslim Baiburs, who controlled the Holy City. Edward was preparing to continue his own campaign when he was attacked by an assassin, who stabbed him in the arm before being killed. Although the assassination failed, Edward was severely weakened, possibly by poison from the tip of the dagger, and had to abandon his campaign.

The assassins lasted in Syria for another century, continuing to be hired by Mamluks, but then they dissipated. Nonetheless, they are rumored to have been behind countless other assassinations, and there are numerous myths about their continued existence as a secret order.

Whatever the fate of the assassins, the Nizari Ismaili went from strength to strength. Today, it is the second largest Shia religion, with over 15 million adherents across the world. The present Imam is His Highness Prince Shah Karim Al-Husayni, the Aga Khan IV.

Opposite: Richard the Lionheart, the English king depicted in an equestrian statue in Parliament Square, London, was rumored to have hired the assassins to kill the King of Jerusalem in 1192

Samurai

The Japanese medieval military nobility, known for their strict code of honor and magnificent swordsmanship

THERE IS NO more enduring image of the noble but fearsome warrior than that of the samurai, dressed in elaborately designed armor and carrying the famed samurai sword—the katana. Given extra kudos by their strict code of honor, they have become the legendary figures of medieval warfare in the East—chivalrous, disciplined, skilled, and merciless.

Samurai derives from the Japanese word *saburau*, which describes one who serves the nobility, but does not mean a soldier. Over time, the samurai became exclusively *bushi* ("warriors"), drawn from the middle and upper classes, and their way of life and personal code of chivalry is known as *bushido* ("the way of the warrior"). Within the course of a few centuries, they had stopped serving the nobility: they had become the nobility.

Samurai warriors emerged in the closing centuries of the first millennium. Known as fearsome and talented fighters, they would be hired by provincial governors as a bodyguard and as enforcers in local disputes or for tax collection. Noble families and temples would also hire samurai to protect their estates from their neighbors, over-greedy governors and

FACT FILE

COUNTRY: Japan

ERA: 9th to 19th century

KEY ENCOUNTERS: Gempai War 1180-85; Kamakura Shogunate 1185; Onin War 1467-77; Nobunaga ends Ashikaga Shogunate 1573

TACTICS AND TECHNIQUES: Originally mounted archers, later highly trained swordsmen who followed a strict code of honor

WEAPONRY: *Katana* sword, spear, longbow, club, matchlock

LEGACY: Warriors who became noble rulers, famed for their skill and chivalry

Above: The Heiji Scroll showing the night attack on Sanjo Palace during the Heiji rebellion of 1159

magistrates, and so warriors would find themselves fighting on opposite sides of a dispute. They became key figures in the provincial militarization of Japan, reaping significant income from local conflicts.

Wealthy lineages of samurai emerged in the 12th century, and they began to gain both prestige and influence. Two of the most notable samurai families or clans were the Taira and Minamoto, who had networks of warriors at their disposal and gained affiliations in the imperial court. During the Hogen Rebellion of 1156, in which there was a dispute for the succession of imperial power, the fate of Japan lay in the hands of these warrior clans, who warred amongst themselves with some supporting Emperor Sutoku and others supporting Emperor Go-Shirakawa.

These were early days in the great tradition of the samurai, but one might still expect that superior and elegant combat skills won the day; nothing could be further from the truth. After Minamoto no Yoshitomo had seen his attack on Sanjo Palace repulsed by the superior archery units of his younger brother, he took the easy option and set the palace on fire.

Sutoku's samurai fled or were slaughtered amid the scenes of carnage that followed. The secret to the success of the samurai lay not just in their code of honor or skill, but in their political connivance and mercilessness.

The Minamoto and Taira clans were directly opposed to each other in the Heiji Rebellion of 1159, and a full civil war became inevitable. Starting in 1180, the Gempei War as it was known lasted for five years. Most of the battles involved only a few hundred samurai—this was a war conducted exclusively between highly trained, elite warriors, not conscripted foot soldiers. They primarily fought as mounted archers and were yet to become the famed swordsmen of legend, preferring to use the bow from a distance rather than meet in close combat. However, the distinctive samurai armor of small overlapping plates, made of iron or leather and threaded together with cords, was already established. The sectioning of the armor into plates aided flexibility of movement and helped deflect arrows.

In the interim between the Heiji Rebellion and the Genpei War, the Taira had gained power but lost focus as a military force, having become too embroiled in the orthodoxies of civilian administration. In contrast the Minamoto were stronger and better trained than ever, with new clan leader Yoritomo sharing his father's ruthlessness and ambition, and allying it with the added bonus of military acumen. After the Minamoto crushed the Taira in 1185, the imperial court conferred the honorific title of shogun—"general"—on Minamoto no Yoritomo. With no great rival, he established a warrior government, the Kamakura Shogunate, and in terms of real power the imperial government in Kyoto became an irrelevance: the warrior class were now the masters of the aristocracy. The age of the samurai had truly arrived.

The stranglehold that the Kamakura Shogunate had on Japan lasted for almost 150 years. During this period, samurai began to take on the ways of the nobility, learning calligraphy and appreciating the fine arts. They also adopted Zen Buddhism, which helped imbue the warriors with some of the characteristics for which they are still famed today: their fearlessness in the face of death and their devoutly followed code of conduct. The warriors were no longer ruthless, hired barbarians: they were now an hereditary elite practicing the art of warfare.

Until 1331, the biggest threat to the Kamakura Shogunate, in which the Hojo clan had become dominant, had been the attempted invasions of the

Opposite: Armor varied in design, materials, ornamentation, and quality according to the wealth and prestige of the samurai; metal plate largely replaced leather in later centuries

Above: Samurai weapons and armor including a fur-covered quiver (right) from the Edo period (1603–1867)

Mongol Yuan Dynasty of China, which were repelled toward the end of the 13th century. A new threat came from within the borders of Japan, when Emperor Go-Daigo united other major samurai families in resistance to the Shogunate. The Hojo defense was led by Ashikaga Takauji, but he changed sides to support Go-Daigo. The imperial forces were on the edge of victory in 1333, when almost 900 Hojo samurai, believing the end was inevitable, committed suicide in the family temple, Tocho-ji.

The resumption of imperial power was not to last. Ashikaga established another warrior government, this time in Kyoto, just a few years later in 1338. The Ashikaga Shogunate became the major power in Japan until 1573, although it was troubled by fierce inter-state warfare.

The samurai's tools and techniques changed over the centuries, especially during the ten-year Onin War, which was waged from 1467. The early samurai may have preferred to work as mounted archers but they had always carried either an almost straight blade called a *katana* or a more curved sword, the *tachi*. The famed samurai sword—highly crafted, sharp and powerful—soon began to play a key role, especially after the structural innovation of a swordsmith named Masamune early in the 14th century. The secret formula he unearthed combined layers of hard and soft steel, which gave a refined, thin blade an awesomely powerful cut.

Samurai were often intent on displaying individual prowess in battle, rather than the swift achievement of a collective objective. However, in the era of warring states, the need for larger armies grew and commanders now used foot soldiers in great numbers, organizing them in disciplined divisions rather than relying on the more idiosyncratic fighting style of individual samurai. The weapon of first contact became the spear, before swords were drawn. By the middle of the 16th century, following the opening up of trade with Europe, the warriors had even adopted the use of that most un-samurai-like weapon: the matchlock gun. As a result plate armor became more common.

The samurai now had to sacrifice personal ego to the greater good, and this became a fundamental element of the *bushido*, the way of the warrior. They would no longer rush into battle in order to be seen as a hero, or deliberately line themselves up in one-to-one combat with the enemy's best warriors so they could prove their superior skill. The code was severe and restrictive, but it enhanced their reputation, allowing them to inhabit

THE WAY OF THE WARRIOR

IN 1582, THE samurai general Akashi Gidayu sat on the floor, wrote a death poem, and then used a short blade called a *tanto* to commit *seppuku*—suicide by disembowelment, often referred to as *hara-kiri*. He had disgraced his master by being defeated in battle and followed "the way of the warrior" by killing himself in shame. The code of the samurai or *bushido* became fully established in the 15th and 16th centuries. As the samurai Kato Kiyomasa wrote at the time: "If a man does not investigate into the matter of *bushido* daily, it will be difficult for him to die a brave and manly death. Thus it is essential to engrave this business of the warrior into one's mind well." Linked to Zen Buddhism, the code's principles were loyalty, honor and self-sacrifice. To remain living when you had failed in your duty was a disgrace to the nobility of the samurai.

Above: Samurai wore many types of kabuto (helmets) from rudimentary, horned ones to works of high craftsmanship

their growing status as noble warriors. Codes regulating the behavior of the warriors had been in existence since the 13th century, but more precise and detailed codes evolved during the Ashikaga Shogunate. At their core lay the virtue of self-sacrifice: as the samurai lord Shiba Yoshimasa declared, "It is a matter of regret to let the moment when one should die pass by."

The Battle of Okehazama in 1560 demonstrated the martial abilities of a band of accomplished samurai against a far larger army, and revealed just why discipline was the key to martial success. The Imagawa family was a powerful offshoot of the Ashikaga and, following several skirmishes, decided to extinguish the irritating threat of the neighboring Nobunaga, a less notable family. The Imagawa gathered an impressive force of 20,000 warriors under the command of Imagawa Yoshimoto, and attacked two forts on Oda territory in a deliberately provocative move. Oda Nobunaga could only raise about a quarter of the number of men, but nonetheless decided to meet Yoshimoto's force head-on.

In the midst of torrential rain Nobunaga came across the Yoshimoto vanguard. They were resting, waiting for the remainder of the army, and failed to heed the instruction found in codes such as *The Fundamental Laws of Kai Province*, issued by a leading samurai in 1547: "it is of the utmost importance to keep one's military equipment at the ready."

Nobunaga launched a stunning surprise attack. Amid the rain and ensuing confusion, Yoshimoto was slain and his forces were routed by Nobunaga's smaller band of more disciplined and skilled warriors. At the end of the battle, the fortunes of the Imagawa family lay bloodstained in the mud. In 1573, Oda Nobunaga captured Kyoto and ousted the Ashikaga. Despite the high social status the samurai class had gained over the centuries, there was still no better route to power than through the surgical application of cold steel.

Above: Samurai blade with marks made by the blacksmith

Nobunaga put an end to the era of warring states, and Japan entered a time of more settled, civilian administration during the Tokugawa Shogunate, which lasted until 1868.

In an era of peace, the importance of the samurai diminished and the imperial court effectively regained power. Modern warfare had also left the role of the samurai behind. In 1873 Emperor Meiji abolished the samurai's right to be the sole force allowed to bear arms, and replaced them with a conscripted army trained for modern warfare. The world was changing rapidly, and Japan had to be ready to face a new era of international conflict.

The samurai faded in importance, but the legend was set in stone. Today, there remains a deep fascination with the samurai code, weaponry, and armor.

Knights Templar

The secretive religious order of noblemen who rose to power in the Crusades, and spread throughout Europe

"HASTEN THEN TO expiate your sins by victories over the infidels, and let the deliverance of the holy places be the reward of your repentance ... Fly then to arms; let a holy rage animate you in the fight, and let the Christian world resound with these words of the prophet, 'Cursed be he who does not stain his sword with blood.'"

With these words, St Bernard of Clairvaux invoked the knights of France to join the Second Crusade to the Holy Land in 1146. One group of nobles who needed no such cajoling were the Poor Fellow Soldiers of Christ and the Temple of Solomon, otherwise known as the Knights Templar, the secretive band of monk-soldiers who viewed the slaying of their religious enemies as their life's work. Supposedly the saviors of Christianity, they were eventually burned at the stake for heresy. The secret order was feared not just in the Holy Land, but by their fellow French, who believed its members were conspiring against both Church and State.

Religion may be the cause of many wars, but the soldiers of such conflicts are rarely the devout members of a religious order. The Knights Templar, unusually, were both a religious and military elite, devoted to Christianity and to its martial protection.

FACT FILE

REGION: France and the Middle East
ERA: c.1120–1312
KEY ENCOUNTERS: Council of Troyes 1128–9; Battle of Arsuf 1191; Battle of La Forbie 1244; Capture of Acre 1291
TACTICS AND TECHNIQUES: Mounted knights, used in most exposed sections of battle formations
WEAPONRY: Lance, sword, and shield
LEGACY: Warrior-monks of the Crusades who remain the subject of conspiracy theories

The Templars were officially sanctioned by the Catholic Church in 1128–29 but had already secretly been in existence for up to 30 years.

They were originally a fraternity composed of a handful of very pious French knights led by Hugues de Payens. Jerusalem had been captured by the knights of the First Crusade in 1099, and twenty years later the al-Aqsa mosque, which was believed to be the ancient Temple of Solomon, was given to the Knights Templar. In exchange the knights had probably taken vows to remain loyal to King Baldwin, the Patriarch of Jerusalem appointed by the West. At this point, despite being given one of the most important religious buildings in the Holy Land, the Templars were unknown in France. At first they were possibly quite genuinely poor and relied on charitable handouts, with their poverty expressed in their symbol of two knights riding on a single horse. However, such claims to poverty ceased to be valid almost immediately after the Council of Troyes in 1128–29.

The future saint Bernard, abbot of Clairvaux, announced that the Temple was now an officially endorsed religious order. He also wrote a tract, *In Praise of the New Knighthood*, and gave the Temple its Rule. This set of laws bound

Below: A 14th-century castle of the Knights Hospitaller on the island of Kos. The Hospitallers sometime fought alongside the Knights Templar and maintained a presence in the Mediterranean for most of the last millennium

Above: Chainmail typically worn by the Templars despite the heat of battle in the Middle East

the knights to be highly disciplined, armored defendants of Christ. Among some rather peculiar and exacting clauses—such as the banning of pointed shoes, shoelaces, and ornate bridles—was the vital phrase "this armed company of knights may kill the enemies of the cross without sinning." Somewhat in contradiction to the "Poor Fellow" aspect of the Templar's title, he allowed the knights to have land and servants, and to collect tithes.

The publicity gained from Bernard's advocacy could not have been better. There was no greater uniting mission in the Christian West than the preservation of the Holy Land, free from Muslim hands (even though Jerusalem is a holy city of Islam). The sons of wealthy families joined the order, and the Templars began to receive huge financial donations and lands for their work in the East. It is the huge donations the Templars received, and their consequent financial manipulation of those funds, that has spurred on many conspiracy theories about the order.

Soon the "Poor" Fellow Soldiers were not poor at all. These were rich knights who were not only able to fund their hugely expensive

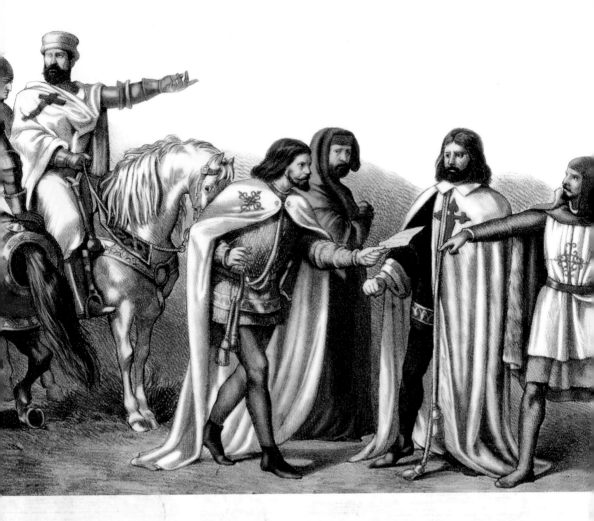

religio-military enterprises in the Middle East, but effectively became a major financial institution in Europe. The order soon included non-combatants who regulated the funds, forming an innovative and successful early form of banking that increased the Temple's power and influence. In 1139, the financial prospects of the order were further improved by a papal bull issued by Innocent II, making the order exempt from taxation. Over the decades, many leading figures across Europe became financially indebted to the order.

It was not only the order's piety that was respected, but its knights' military abilities. During the Second Crusade, which began in 1146, King Louis VII of France placed divisions of his army directly under the command of the Templars. Like all knights of the period, they were

Above: A gathering of knights including the Knights Templar (on horseback) and the Spanish orders of Alcántara, Calatrava and Santiago, whose mission was to fight against Muslim control of Spain

Above: The Knights Templar, who fought in the Holy Land for almost 200 years

equipped with a lance, sword, and shield, as well as chainmail, which must have proved draining in the heat of battle in the Middle East. High levels of discipline and organization, as laid down by their Rule, made the knights distinct from their counterparts, as did their white tunics adorned by a red cross over their armor.

By 1170, the small band of the Knights Templar had expanded to several hundred, with many more non-combatant bankers remaining back home in Europe to manage their burgeoning financial infrastructure. By the 13th century there were ten times as many administrators in the order as there were knights. The Temple began to issue credit notes to knights and pilgrims, who would deposit their wealth with the Temple while in the Holy Land. The clients would then be able to trade using the credit notes, and thus a very early form of banking and a nascent international financial institution was created.

The Temple acquired swathes of land across Europe, and the historic legal centre of English law, comprising the Middle and Inner Temples, is still named after the order's holdings in London, England. The Round Church of London's Temple Church, which was built by the Templars in 1185 and still stands today, was designed to recall the Church of the Holy Sepulcher in Jerusalem.

In battle the Templars were aided by divisions of infantry and light cavalry in the form of Turcopoles, and usually led the armies of the Crusades in a charged assault on the enemy. In 1177 at the Battle of Montgisard, the Templars spearheaded one of the greatest victories of the Western Crusaders in the Middle East. A company of less than 500 mounted Templars and a few thousand infantry defeated an army of more than 25,000 soldiers led by Saladin—the Sultan of Syria and Egypt, who was the greatest military leader of the whole Crusader era.

The Templars were brave but could also be foolhardy in their pursuit of victory. In May 1187, a force of just 140 Templars and knights from another soldier-monk order, the Hospital of St John of Jerusalem, attacked an army of more than 5,000 Muslims at Cresson, near Nazareth. The Master of the Temple, Gerard de Ridefort, allegedly goaded the Hospitallers into fighting, saying to their Master, "You love your blond hair too well to want to lose it!" The results were disastrous. Every Hospitaller knight that took to the field that day was slaughtered; only Gerard and a handful of Templars survived.

ELITE ORDERS OF KNIGHTS

THE KNIGHTS TEMPLAR were only one amongst several elite orders of religious knights in the medieval era. The most long-standing were the Hospital of St John of Jerusalem, known as the Hospitallers, who emerged around the same time as the Templars and also fought in the Holy Land. After the Temple was officially dissolved, the Pope gave many of its assets to the Hospitallers, who had seized Rhodes in 1310 and remained there for hundreds of years as a thorn in the side of the Ottoman Empire. The Order of Calatrava, a sect of monk-soldiers directly inspired by the Knights Templar, was formed in 1164 for the reconquest of Spain from the Moors. Meanwhile, the Teutonic Order— or, more grandly, the Order of the Hospital of St Mary of the Germans of Jerusalem—was established in 1191, andbecame a major force in Prussia and the Baltic for over 200 years.

Saladin crushed the Crusaders at the Battle of the Horns of Hattin later that year and captured Jerusalem. After Montgisard and other battles, Saladin was all too aware of the prowess of the Templars. Consequently, he had every Templar prisoner executed. The remaining knights had to flee the Temple of Solomon.

The Templars soon recovered as a fighting force. Richard the Lionheart, King of England, had a great deal of faith in the fighting ability of the warrior-monks, who helped him capture Acre in 1189. He then marched his army towards Jaffa, protecting his knights by surrounding them with infantry and archers. However, the vanguard of the column was particularly vulnerable, so he chose to place the Knights Templar at the front. They were happy to oblige—after all, as their religious patron Bernard of Clairvaux once said, "How blessed are the martyrs who die in battle." When the column reached Arsuf, Saladin preferred to assault the Hospitallers at the army's rear rather than face the Templars head on. The Crusaders proved victorious and Jaffa became an important stronghold, but their inability to recapture Jerusalem dealt a death blow to their ambitions in the Holy Land. The Knights Templar were forced to take up permanent residence in Acre.

The Templars continued to be a presence in the Middle East over the next century but suffered a massive loss at the Battle of La Forbie in 1244, losing 600 knights—almost the entire order. They were soon slaughtered again, this time at Mansurah in 1250.

Time and time again, the Knights Templar, despite their setbacks, proved that they were the West's most elite unit in the Middle East and were willing to take up the most vulnerable positions on the battlefield, relying on a mixture of their training, chivalric valor, and unstinting religious fervor. They were also essential in the West's attempts to maintain a permanent foothold in the Holy Land; the Temple strengthened the fortress at Baghras

Above: The 13th-century poet Tannhauser is depicted in the courtly robes of a Teutonic knight in the Codex Manesse (c.1304), suggesting he may have fought in the Crusades

Opposite: Temple Church, established by the Knights Templar in 1185, is in the heart of London, England

in Antioch and built the Crusader citadel at Atlit. In Europe many churches and other buildings were built or restored by the Temple, funded by their unusual financial dealings.

With the loss of Acre in 1291, the Temple could no longer maintain a footing in the Holy Land and lost its remaining strongholds, including Atlit. The Templars were forced to flee the Middle East and found a safe haven in Cyprus. Without the Crusades and the mission in the Holy Land, the order became ideologically irrelevant, and questions and conspiracies theories rose about the secretive, inordinately rich Poor Fellow Soldiers. Their financial power had become so great within Europe that even the King of France, Philip IV, had borrowed a huge sum of money from them in order to conduct a war with England.

Below: A hooded Knight Templar bears the symbol of the cross on his breastplate to show that he has taken up the cause of the crusade

This was to prove the Temple's undoing. Rather than pay back his debts, Philip took advantage of the growing rumors about the Templars. Regarding initiation into the order, the Temple's Rule included the instruction to "Test the soul to see if it comes from God." To this day, no one knows exactly what these "tests" involved, but Philip accused the Knights Templar of obscene rituals, idolatry, heresy, and sexual deviancy. An arrest warrant, featuring the words "God is not pleased. We have enemies of the faith in the kingdom," was issued in 1307, and many knights, including their Grand Master Jacques de Molay, were rounded up.

Pope Clement was bullied by Philip into declaring that it was the duty of all Christian monarchs to arrest the Templars and confiscate their assets. Many Templars confessed under extreme torture, even saying that they had urinated on the cross, and over 50 Templars were burned at the stake in 1310. As a result of the confessions, Pope Clement officially dissolved the order of the Poor Fellow Soldiers of Christ and the Temple of Solomon by papal decree in 1312, even though the Church's Council of

Vienne refused to convict the Templars of heresy. Some of the knights, including de Molay, retracted their confessions.

The last Grand Master of the order was led to the stake with fellow Templar Geoffroi de Charney in Paris in March 1314. He made one final confession: "my crime is this: that I confessed to malicious charges made against an order that is innocent so that I could escape further torture. I shall not confirm a first lie with a second. I renounce life willingly." Then, according to legend, just before he was burned alive de Molay said that within a year and a day, Philip IV and Pope Clement would be called upon to answer for their actions before God. Whether as a direct result of the curse of not, both Philip and Clement were dead before the end of the year.

In the meantime, if Philip's intention had been to get his hands on the Temple's huge wealth, he was to be disappointed. The papacy directed much of the money to the Hospitallers, who became an irritant to the empire of the Ottoman Turks for centuries. Nor were all the Templars arrested, and it seems certain that at least part of the order's assets was hidden to protect it from seizure.

Above: Jacques de Molay, Grand Master of the Knights Templar, was burned at the stake for heresy in 1314

The remaining Templars completely disappeared from view, leading to rumors that the order merely went underground, and continues secretly to exert power and influence to this very day. Freemasonry is strongly linked to the Temple, borrowing elements of its structure, symbols, rituals, and, supposedly, its secret initiation ceremony, from the Poor Fellow Soldiers of Christ and the Temple of Solomon. Meanwhile, tales of the Holy Grail and the Turin Shroud have become entwined with the legends of the mysterious order of the Temple.

Janissaries

The personal bodyguard and household infantry of the ruler of the mighty Muslim Ottoman Empire

THE 12 YEAR-OLD Slav Christian boy barely looked up when he reached the front of the queue. Within the next two minutes he would be ripped from the grasp of his mother by the agents of the Sultan and dragged away. He would never see his family again. He and hundreds of other young Christian boys would be marched on foot to Bursa, the Ottoman capital, a vast distance away. On arrival, those who survived the journey were circumcised. The boy was now a trainee soldier of the Janissaries, the finest elite unit of the Muslim army of the Ottoman Empire. In time he would fight to the death for the Sultan.

FACT FILE

REGION: Ottoman Empire

ERA: c.1370–1826

KEY ENCOUNTERS: Siege of Constantinople; Battle of Chaldiran 1514; Battle of Mohács 1526; Auspicious Incident 1826

TACTICS AND TECHNIQUES: Standing army of infantry; early experts in volley-fire and sapping

WEAPONRY: recurve bow; matchlock musket; yatagan saber; grenade and hand-cannon

LEGACY: Essential to the expansion and maintenance of the Ottoman Empire, they ended their existence corrupted and despised

This was the typical experience of boys who were recruited to the Janissaries (whose name derives from *yeni çeri*, the Turkish for "new soldier") at the end of the 14th century. The extreme discipline, skill, and loyalty of the Janissaries—soon ingrained in these boys despite their kidnap into a foreign culture—would prove to be one of the principal secrets to the success of the Ottoman Empire. The Janissary corps effectively became the boys' family, and the Sultan was considered their father.

Above: The combined forces of the Holy Roman Empire rallied against the Ottomans following a two-month siege of Vienna in 1683

The elite household guard of Sultan Murad I was created in the 1370s as one of Europe's first permanent professional armies, although originally it consisted of just a few hundred prisoners of war. The Ottomans were beginning to establish an empire in Turkey, the Balkans and Greece, and threatened the security of the Byzantine Empire and its capital, Constantinople. The Sultan was keen to use all available resources at his disposal, and abandoned the practice of conscripting potentially disloyal prisoners. Instead he wanted to create a disciplined unit in which the soldiers were captured, trained, and indoctrinated from an early age. However, it is against the laws of Islam to enslave a fellow Muslim, so Murad looked towards conquered Christians.

He instituted the *devsirme*, a levy system which would penalize Christian families in villages now under Ottoman rule. From every 40 families,

Above and opposite:
Sultan Sueliman the
Magnificent led the
Ottomans at the Battle
of Mohács, 1526

one 12 to 14 year-old boy would often be taken. On arrival in Bursa, only the most intelligent boys were lucky enough to be accepted into the palace school—and over time became an influential class within the court. The remainder became little more than slave labor for local farming families and were subjected to extremely harsh discipline. The boys would learn the Turkish language and customs, as well as the fundaments of Islam. Once adulthood approached, they would be moved to the Janissaries' barracks to train in the ways of warfare. This child-levy system remained in place for centuries, only dying out in the 17th century. The best future soldiers were levied from the Balkans.

The Janissaries were vital to the expansion of the Ottoman Empire. By 1389, the household infantry unit had already expanded to around 2,000 soldiers, who fought valiantly against the Serbs at the Battle of Kosovo. They proved their worth and, by 1500, future sultans would increase the regiment's numbers to 20,000, including almost 8,000 novices. To have such a large standing army was unusual and expensive, but it was an essential tool in the armory of the Empire. Despite the child-conscription origins of the force, the soldiers were well paid and issued with new clothing every year. As well as taking to the field and providing the Sultan's bodyguard, they played a vital civic role in peacetime, acting as policemen, firefighters, and nightwatchmen.

In their early years, the Janissaries were highly trained archers, using a powerful recurve bow—with tips that curved away from the bowman—as well as a saber and shield. Each soldier was given a gold piece every year—solely to enable him to replace his bow. The Janissaries became early adopters of firearms in the 15th century, with the troops using muzzle-loaded arquebuses before Murad III had them replaced with matchlock muskets, which many Janissaries continued to use even after the invention of the more reliable flintlock.

In 1453, the troops took part in the most pivotal conflict in the 600-year history of the Ottoman Empire: the siege of Constantinople. It marked the end of the Byzantine Empire and the victorious Ottomans made the city their new capital, which became known as Istanbul.

Around this time, the Janissaries' importance in the battlefield was such that one Serbian Janissary, Konstantin Mihailović, was bold enough to state that "if the imperial Janissaries were once decisively defeated ... the Turkish emperor could never recover." The Sultan himself would lead the Janissaries into battle, and they took part in every major campaign undertaken by the burgeoning Ottoman Empire. In his memoirs, Mihailović describes Memhed II and the Janissaries making progress in Eastern Europe: "we drove all the army from the battlefield and established and fortified ourselves ... Then the emperor himself with all his might crossed the Danube and there gave us 30,000 gold pieces to divide among ourselves."

The Janissaries played a vital role at the Battles of Chaldiran in 1514, when the Ottomans defeated the Safavid Empire in Persia; and the Battles of Marj Dabiq (1516) and Raydaniyya (1517) against the Mamluk Sultanate in Egypt. After Raydaniyya, the head of the Mamluk Sultan was hung from a gate in Cairo. The Janissaries had brought another empire to its knees.

The keys to their success were training, discipline and organization in the field. The laws of the Janissaries included complete obedience to their officers; observance of religious law; abstinence from luxury; permanent

residence in barracks and full-time practice in the arts of war; no marriage; no beards; and no engagement in trade.

They practiced shooting several times a week, and they had already adopted a very advanced technique of volley-firing by the Battle of Mohács in 1526. The Hungarian forces had made great headway and were on the cusp of winning the battle when they found themselves facing the ranks of the Janissaries. Unusually, the Janissaries dispensed with the use of a rest to support a weapon and aid accuracy. The first row of soldiers fired in unison in a standing or kneeling position and reloaded while the second row let loose a volley. The result, as at Mohács, would often be carnage in the ranks of the enemy infantry—the Hungarian kingdom met its demise that day. As well as expert shooters, the force included engineers—sappers who became specialists in the art of explosives—and the troops also favored grenades and the *yatagan*, a short saber, which became the symbol of the unit.

While campaigning, the Janissaries were supported by a highly sophisticated military machine, which was almost unique in warfare at the time. They had a field support unit which would set tents, prepare food, and resupply ammunition and weaponry, and they had mobile hospitals manned by Muslim and Jewish surgeons.

Opposite: The Battle of Mohács, 1526, where the Janissaries used their volley-firing technique to great effect to defeat the Kingdom of Hungary

The Janissaries' tactics and distinctive dress made them the subject of Western fascination and admiration, inspiring such artists as Gentile Bellini to depict them. They wore uniforms woven from wool and distinctive headwear in the form of a woolen cap or *börk*, often with material flowing down the back. They also marched into battle to the sound of the *mehterân*, bands which playing menacing, shrill, and percussive music.

Below: Gentille Bellini's drawing of 1479–81 showed an increasing Western fascination with the Janissaries' costume and weaponry; janissary saber, known as a *yatagan*, and scabbard (bottom)

However, the Janissaries' ascendency in the field was not to last. Their numbers continually increased, but their quality and discipline as an elite unit declined. An early 17th-century version of the laws of the Janissary reported that the soldiers were using their wicks for candles rather than shooting practice, and gunpowder was no longer used in practice drills.

The system of relying on the Christian child-levy had been abandoned and Turkish families were signing up their children so they could enjoy the privileges and status afforded the elite. By the end of that century, the force's number had reached nearly 80,000.

Sultan Murad I's initial concept of a highly loyal elite had almost entirely dissipated. It was impossible for the imperial treasury to maintain this huge standing army, so the soldiers were allowed to take other employment. In the 18th-century, the Janissaries were only paid a nominal fee and many did not live in army barracks. Hordes of them spent their days as craftsmen or shop-keepers, supporting formerly-forbidden wives and families.

With the lack of elite discipline, disloyalty and corruption became endemic in the force. Officers would often keep the names of dead soldiers on the pay-roll and siphon off payments. Whereas once they had policed the major cities fairly and ensured the protection of the civilian populace, the Janissaries had become violent, brutal bullies who extorted money and took bribes. And whereas once they had been provisional firefighters, they allowed Istanbul to burn in the catastrophic fire of 1588, preferring to seize the opportunity to loot.

They insisted on the privileges of an elite, but no longer offered military skill or loyalty in return. They had their own secret agenda—namely the preservation of their own interests. Despite their reputation for loyalty they had a history of interfering in matters of state: they had revolted over pay in 1449 and in 1622 had imprisoned Sultan Osman II when he attempted to neuter their power. By the 18th century they were frequently revolting against the sultan. In 1807, they were even responsible for the regicide of Selim III, having revolted against his bid to modernize the army. The Janissaries now fancied themselves as the kingmakers of the Ottoman Empire, ready to rise up against any sultan who displeased them.

However, Selim III's successor, Mahmud II, was a canny operator. He already had other troops at his disposal when he made his own reforms. The days in which the Janissaries led the way in innovations of modern warfare were far behind them; they were a bloated, costly liability, and no match for the increasingly sophisticated militarism of Western European countries. Selim wanted rid of them altogether.

When the Janissaries revolted in 1826, he announced a fatwa, declaring, "If unjust and violent men attack their brethren, fight against the aggressors and send them before their natural judges." He then set his newly formed professional corps against the Janissaries. Unlike the former elite, his new corps was a disciplined force. In what became known as the Auspicious Incident, the new soldiers assaulted the Janissaries' barracks with a barrage of cannon fire, wiping out around 5,000 of them. Others were hunted down and slain, or imprisoned and later executed. Meanwhile, local populations across the Ottoman Empire, fed up with years of tyranny, rebelled against provincial Janissaries and finally liberated themselves.

By the end of that year, the Janissaries had been destroyed and formally abolished, and the Ottoman military entered a new era.

Ninja

The Japanese specialists in unorthodox warfare, known for assassinations, espionage, and sabotage

Opposite: Tokugawa Ieyasu used ninja warriors in his rise to power, unifying Japan under his shogunate in the 17th century

THE STEALTHY FIGURES—masked and entirely dressed in black—climbed the ropes and spirited across the rooftops, keeping low, before dropping into the courtyard without a sound. In the next two minutes, the local samurai warlord would be killed before he even had time to reach for his sword.

The killers were ninja, the mysterious figures of the Sengoku "warring states" period of Japanese history. While the samurai were known for their nobility, code of honor, and orthodox fighting techniques, the ninja were their dark reflections: masked, secretive, and unorthodox. They were men of the shadows whose identities usually remained hidden, leading them to become both heroes and villains of Japanese folklore.

The literature of the time was more focused on the noble samurai than these lower class, secretive assassins, so their history is subject to greater conjecture. Despite the myths and legends, the ninja, or *shinobi* (which means "to steal away") as they were more commonly known at

FACT FILE

REGION: Japan
ERA: 15th to 17th centuries
KEY ENCOUNTERS: Emergence of ninja training villages 15th century; Destruction of ninja system 1581; Battle of Sekigahara 1600
TACTICS AND TECHNIQUES: Covert operations involving spying, sabotage, and assassination
WEAPONRY: *katana* sword; *shuriken* throwing missiles; grenades and explosives; chain and sickle; poison
LEGACY: Helped sustain the Sengoku period of "warring states" before becoming folkloric symbols of undercover stealth

the time, were genuine historical figures whose actions influenced war and politics in Japan from the 15th to the 17th centuries. The warriors disappeared in the peaceful era of the Tokugawa Shogunate, during which Japan became unified.

The ninja had emerged in nine family clans based in Koga and nearby Iga Province. Each clan had a highly trained fighting unit; whereas samurai manuals are codes of honor, ninja manuals such as the *Bansenshukai* are guides to fighting. The manual was written in 1676, but the ancestors of the ninja stretch back to more than a thousand years earlier. According to the Kojiki chronicle of the 8th century, a 4th-century prince named Yamato Takeru disguised himself as a woman so that he could assassinate two chieftains. Such underhand tactics would become the mark of the ninja, who emerged in the 15th century as trained mercenaries hired for assassinations, spying, surprise attacks, sabotage, and arson. Samurai were available for hire too, but the anonymous *shinobi* were used by the samurai warlords themselves to undertake unconventional, underhand and disreputable acts.

Right: Hokusai depicted Ninja tactics, including abseiling, in 1817, helping to establish the legend of the stealthy fighters camouflaged in black for night attacks

The inaccessible villages amongst the mountains of Koga and Iga became specialist covert-warfare training centers for the ninja family clans, who were made up of lower-class *genin* ("lower men") led by a *jonin* ("upper man") and his assistants, the *chunin* ("middle men"). The *genin* agents were trained from childhood in martial arts, survival, scouting techniques, explosives, and the fine art of murder using weaponry and poisons. Strength and stamina were essential, so physical exercise included long-distance running and climbing—the latter often proved particularly necessary as they undertook their covert operations. Ninja are sometimes depicted as solo agents, but according to historical descriptions they often worked as a team, including when they needed to scale high walls using a human pyramid technique.

Like the Persian assassins and the ninja forefather, Yamato Takeru, disguise was their trademark. There are records of ninja dressing as monks, merchants, or bands of entertainers during covert operations. Hanawa Hokinoichi (1746–1821), who specialized in military history, explained the breadth of their role: having "traveled in disguise to other territories to judge the situation of the enemy," they would "inveigle their way into the midst of the enemy to discover gaps, and enter enemy castles to set them on fire, and carried out assassinations, arriving in secret." He describes ninja as going "into the mountains and [disguising] themselves as firewood gatherers to discover and acquire the news about an enemy's territory." Other chronicles describe them as deliberately wearing the same dress as their intended victims in order to cause as much confusion as possible. However, nija are also often depicted wearing all black for their covert nighttime operations, as portrayed by the great Japanese printmaker, Hokusai, in 1817.

Arson was a forte of the ninja. Yoshitaka, the head of the Rokkaku clan of samurai, hired a ninja unit of 48 Iga agents to set fire to Sawayama Castle, a stronghold of the rival Azai clan, in 1558. To worm their way into the castle without suspicion, the ninja stole a lantern bearing an Azai family crest, copied it onto other lanterns and distributed them amongst the unit. Having gained admittance to the castle with the aid of the replica lanterns, they torched it, giving Yoshitaka a notable success. He was to get his comeuppance a few years later when three Iga ninja were hired by a rival to attack and burn Yoshitaka's own fortress to the ground.

Above: A *kusarigama* or grappling hook, which, like the throwing knives (opposite), were part of the ninja's arsenal of tools and weaponry

The *Bansenshukai* manual gives detailed descriptions of ninja equipment and weaponry. Climbing equipment was essential and included an easily transportable collapsible ladder and hand-held claw-hooks, which were also used as weapons. The *katana* sword was popular amongst ninja as well as samurai, but *shuriken* (which literally means "sword hidden in the hand") such as throwing stars and short blades were also used during covert attacks. The range of weapons also included small bows, the chain and sickle, grenades, poisoned darts, and, later, firearms. More unusual weapons included *metsubushi* ("eye-closers") such as an eggshell filled with pepper, flour, or ground glass to disorientate or blind an attacker. One mythical piece of ninja equipment is the *mizugumo*, which possibly involved wooden shoes and air pockets made of animal hide, and was supposedly used to walk on water.

The heyday of the Koga and Iga ninja clans came during the Ashikaga Shogunate, when regional lords were constantly at war with each other. Oda Nobunaga, a leading samurai who was responsible for ending the period of the "warring states," wiped out the clans toward the end of the sixteenth century, but not before they had played a pivotal role in his own success. Nobunaga defeated the samurai of the powerful Imagawa clan at the Battle of Okehazama in 1560, but still needed to suppress the rest of the clan to ensure peace in the region. According to Hanawa Hokinoichi, Tokugawa Ieyasu, Oda's ally at the time, hired a unit of 80 Koga ninja to infiltrate an Imagawa fortress, set fire to it and wipe out its garrison. The ninja duly obliged. Nobunaga himself reputedly hired the ninja Hachisuka Tenzo to kill a powerful lord, Takeda Shingen, but the plot failed.

While Nobunaga may have hired ninja, he was all too aware that the spies and assassins had been responsible for much disruption in 16th-century Japan and that their removal was essential to the unification of the country. In 1571, a ninja named Sugitani Zenjubo fired two shots at him but failing to kill him. Nobunaga survived at least two further ninja assassination attempts, one allegedly involving a plot to carefully drop poison into his mouth from a hole in the ceiling as he slept. In 1581,

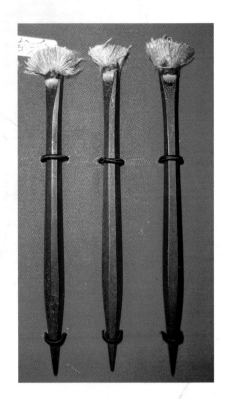

Above: Ninja *shuriken* throwing knives

he sent 40,000 troops into Iga Province, destroyed ninja villages and broke the clans. The Koga network of clans also suffered and the organized ninja training system was eradicated, with ninja fleeing to other regions.

The golden age of the ninja was over but the future shogun Tokugawa Ieyasu still considered them a useful tool, and he continued to hire both Koga and Iga agents in his rise to power. His ally, the powerful samurai Hattori Hanzo, was from a ninja clan in Iga and hired his clansmen as guards at the Edo Palace. Hundreds of Koga played a role in the pivotal Battle of Sekigahara in 1600, which helped Tokugawa stabilize power and unite Japan under his shogunate. Ninja are barely mentioned again in the histories of the period, with the exception of their use to capture Hara Castle in 1638 and put an end to the Shimabara Rebellion, a Christian uprising.

Long-term, the genuine ninja may have returned to the shadows, but their influence remained in the form of the Oniwabanshu, the network of undercover agents that emerged in the peaceful years of the Tokugawa Shogunate. The nimble, light-footed and highly trained spies and assassins have remained a significant part of Japanese folklore.

Streltsy

Ivan the Terrible's marksmen, known as the "Shooters," who became the elite of the Russian army in the 16th century

WHILE THE JANISSARIES were demonstrating the growing importance of firearms during the expansion of the Ottoman Empire, Ivan the Terrible was all too well aware that Russia's infantry was not cut out for modern warfare, which had developed at an extraordinary rate in the 15th and 16th centuries. As a result he created an elite force, which in time would become both a blessing and a curse to the fortunes of the Russian Empire.

Ivan the Terrible, who became Tsar of All the Russias in 1547, earned his epithet. He was known for his terrifying anger, episodes of mental illness, and mercilessness in his desire to expand the boundaries of Russia. Yet he was not an unintelligent ogre: he was learned and religiously devout, and initiated impressive administrative reforms. As a leader, he began the transformation of Russia from a medieval, barbaric collection of disunited lands into one of the world's greatest empires. And his most effective secret tool would prove to be the Streltsy.

Rather than small firearms, the Russians preferred to use heavy firepower to create a bombardment from strongly

FACT FILE

REGION: Russian Empire

ERA: 1551–1700

KEY ENCOUNTERS: Capture of Kazan 1552; Siege of Pskov 1581–2; Moscow Uprising 1682; Streltsy Uprising 1698

TACTICS AND TECHNIQUES: Household infantry of sharp-shooters adept at defending fixed positions behind palisades

WEAPONRY: Musket; *berdysh* long-handled ax; saber

LEGACY: Helped to establish and defend the Russian Empire

defended positions, but they were leaden-footed in open battle. The Streltsy were Tsar Ivan's elegant solution to this. First established in 1551 as the tsar's elite personal bodyguard, their name means "the shooters." They became a light infantry unit that combined modern innovation with more traditional weaponry: in one hand they carried a musket, while in the other was a *berdysh*, a long-handled ax with a blade in the shape of a crescent moon. The axes were not only effective weapons in close combat; the Streltsy also used them as rests to aid the legendary accuracy of the musketeers.

Recruited from free-born Russians at a time when serfs made up the majority of the population, the Streltsy soon became an honorable and distinctive unit. Its numbers grew rapidly from 3,000 to almost ten times that by the end of the 16th century. Each regiment wore long kaftans in blue, red, or green, adorned with contrasting braid, together with yellow boots and a fur hat.

Ivan the Terrible had taken a leaf out of the book of the Ottoman sultans: like the Janissaries, the Streltsy were a professional, well-trained standing army at a time when monarchs usually raised militia on an ad-hoc basis in the face of war. However, what Ivan failed to learn was that an elite household force could soon start to flex its muscles on the home front. Just like the Janissaries, the Streltsy would become more obsessed with their own privileges and status than the safety of their anointed leader, and would start to play dangerous political games with the future of Russia.

In the meantime, the Streltsy would be an invaluable asset on the battlefield. In 1552, just a year after their creation, they were involved in the capture of Kazan. Four years later, they helped Ivan defeat the khanate of Astrakhan, and in 1563 they were instrumental in the capture of Polotsk. This pivotal encounter opened the gateway for the overrunning of Livonia, allowing the Russians to—at least temporarily—push their empire westwards towards the Baltic Sea. During battle, the Streltsy would undertake the increasingly vital role of the light infantry, while the nobles (known as Boyars) and Cossacks would lead the cavalry. Additional foot soldiers came in the form of a non-professional militia.

The Moscow regiment of the Streltsy was the elite of the elite, numbering approximately 2,800 soldiers by 1600. They had particular responsibility for guarding the Tsar in the Kremlin, and were able to maneuver themselves into positions of influence in his court. In peacetime, the Streltsy acted as a police force, garrisoning fortresses across the burgeoning empire to make sure that no popular discontent could gain momentum.

During the expansion of the Russian Empire, the Streltsy became particularly adept at siege warfare. The 1581-82 Siege of Pskov in the midst of the Livonian War proved a notable success. The Poles had started to counterattack against the Russian advance, retaking Livonia and surging forward to threaten the borders of Russia itself. Holding the city of Pskov became strategically vital, so 7,000 Streltsy, 10,000 militia, and 2,000 cavalry set up camp to defend it from the Poles. The siege lasted for five bitter winter months over the course of winter, but the Streltsy held firm. Their resilience during this period gave Ivan the Terrible enough time to reach a vital settlement with the enemy.

This proved to be one of the final significant acts of Ivan's reign. On 28 March 1584 he died from a stroke while playing chess. As Ivan's personal

Opposite: Ivan the Terrible, the feared Russian leader, wanted an elite, professional army, but the Streltsy would eventually threaten their own masters

Below: The Streltsy, seen here in an illustration from 1674, used the *berdysh* (above and right), a long-handled ax, both as a fearsome weapon and as a gun rest to improve the accuracy of their shooting

guard, the Streltsy may have feared for their role following his death. Furthermore, they had never really become the superior, maneuverable, attacking force that Ivan may have originally envisaged, proving far more adept at fighting in static formations to maintain defensive positions. However, over the course of the next century, the unit would continue to grow in both size and power, and like the Janissaries, would be utterly hostile to change.

Elements of the Russian army developed in the 1630s to combat the increasingly well-organized, European-style infantry of the Poles, who used a combination of pike and shot. However, the Streltsy refused to reform. At the root of the Streltsy's obstreperousness was the unit's self-regard as a military and social elite. They thought themselves superior to the common infantrymen, and were not going to change their noble ways. Self-interest, rather than the interests of the Empire, was beginning to get the upper hand. As one foreign visitor reported: "They are most insolent ... and inspire the greatest fear in Moscow."

Toward the end of the 17th century, the Streltsy became increasingly involved in domestic politics. Rather than acting as the neutral servants of the incumbent tsar, they were now attempting to shape the political destiny of the Empire. By 1682, they were a flabby and malcontent force of 55,000 men, and were set against any modern or "foreign" innovations.

The imperial succession had become complicated following the death of Tsar Feodor III in April of that year. His infirm brother Ivan, aged 15, was first in line to the throne, but the Patriarch of the Russian Orthodox Church proclaimed his half-brother Peter, aged nine, as Tsar. Ivan's supporters then claimed that those supporting Peter had strangled the sickly Ivan in the Kremlin.

The Streltsy took up Ivan's cause and stormed the Kremlin. Once there, they ran riot and lynched some of the Boyars and military leaders they accused of corruption and delaying payment of their salaries. Not content with that, they raided the royal residence and killed some of Peter's supporters in front of him, including two of his uncles. Chaos ensued as the Streltsy then joined the impoverished lower classes on the streets of Moscow in a full-scale riot.

Consequently, the "miraculously" unharmed Ivan was proclaimed as the leading tsar of a joint tsardom with Peter, with Ivan's older sister Sophia Alekseyevna given the role of regent on behalf of both boys. The younger brother was forced to spend much of his time away from Moscow to keep support for his claim to the throne from gaining momentum.

Above: While most rulers of the era could not afford professional standing armies, Ivan used his great wealth to support the Streltsy

THE COSSACKS

THE COSSACKS WERE a military-minded people who emerged in Ukraine and became a legendary, elite light cavalry in the service of Peter the Great as he pushed out the frontiers of the Russian Empire. Acclaimed for their horsemanship, they fought in almost every major Russian campaign from the 17th to the 20th centuries, becoming a privileged military caste. They remain famous for their cavalry raid on Berlin in 1760 and their attacks on Napoleon's forces during his attempted invasion of 1812. Cossack means "adventurous or free person" and they resisted both imperial and Soviet attempts to make them conform. Their Russian military role only died out with the final demise of cavalry in World War II.

Sophia was a great power-monger who all along had manipulated the Moscow Uprising alongside the Streltsy's Moscow commander, Prince Ivan Andreyevich Khovansky. But the commander proved to be just as conniving and ambitious as Sophia, and conspired with the Streltsy in an attempt to establish himself as regent. Sophia and her entourage had to flee the Kremlin in the fall until another ally, Fyodor Shaklovity, was able to restore order and assume command of the Muscovite Streltsy. Khovansky was duly executed.

Shaklovity tried to ensure that the Streltsy remained loyal to Sophia. He and the leading Streltsy officers campaigned for Sophia's full coronation and in 1689 conspired to assassinate Peter, who escaped to a monastery thanks to a tip-off from a disloyal Streltsy officer. However, Peter had not been idling away his time during the regency. He had created his own bodyguard and ensured that thee men were trained to the highest Western standards. Following the failed assassination, Peter led a successful counter-coup against Sophia and her Streltsy supporters, and dismantled the regency.

Peter was a great student of Western military, administrative and economic systems, so when he decided to remove the Streltsy, it was not just because of their support for Sophia. He viewed them as an outdated, outmoded unit that had failed to adapt to the innovations of warfare, and he started to introduce more modern—and loyal—units.

The Streltsy were used to being treated with more respect and, having been marginalized and mistreated during Peter's Azov campaign, they took the opportunity to mount a major rebellion in Moscow in 1698. Their ultimate aim was to reinstate Sophia while Peter was touring Western Europe. Peter's loyal general, the Scot Patrick Gordon, met them with force: "They rejected all proposals of compromise, and boasted that they were as ready to defend themselves by force as we were to attack. Seeing that all hope of their submission was vain, I made a round of the cannon be fired." In truth, the Streltsy were no longer elite in military terms; Gordon crushed them.

Above: A bust of Peter the Great, whose reign brought an end to the Streltsy's power

Gordon described the end of the uprising to Peter: "Twenty-four individuals were found guilty, on their own confession, of the most shocking crimes, and of having designed, when they got to Moscow, to massacre certain Boyars, and to extort an increase of pay, and a new regulation of their services." Thousands of Streltsy were gruesomely tortured, executed or sent to garrisons in the far reaches of the Empire. A few Streltsy regiments remained after the uprising but proved completely ineffectual against the superior Swedes at the Battle of Narva in 1700. The pitiful residue of the once mighty force was absorbed into the main army as Peter continued his mission to create a force fit for the modern era.

Yet another elite guard had become corrupted and bloated by power and had collapsed when political fortunes and military innovations made them little more than an overweight, unnecessary liability.

Rogers' Rangers

The scouting arm of the British forces in the French and Indian War of the 1750s, using revolutionary covert tactics to achieve victory

"MOVE FAST AND hit hard," Robert Rogers instructed his men on 6 October 1759. At his signal, 140 hand-picked fighters swept into the village of the Abenaki tribe, whose warriors were held responsible for the deaths of more than 600 colonials in the French and Indian War. Earlier, the Native Americans had apparently subjected British officers to ritual torture. The British force in America required unconventional guerilla tactics, and Rogers was just the man to lead the mission. The surprise attack on the village in the heart of Indian country worked: over 200 Abenaki were killed.

Rogers' Rangers were not the first rangers to be active on American soil, but they would soon become a famous and highly respected elite fighting unit specializing in unconventional warfare. Mobile, lightly armed, and self-sufficient, they were able to work in enemy territory without support. They were the forefathers of the American Green Berets.

Major Robert Rogers of New Hampshire set up the Ranger companies in 1756, two years into the French and Indian War, which the British colonials would fight against their twin enemies on North American

FACT FILE

REGION: North America
ERA: 1756–63
KEY ENCOUNTERS: First and Second Battle on Snowshoes 1757–8; St Francis Raid 1759; Capture of Fort Detroit 1760
TACTICS AND TECHNIQUES: Covert reconnaissance and raids into enemy territory, enduring harsh conditions
WEAPONRY: Flintlock musket; hatchet, knife
LEGACY: Helped the British defeat the French and Indians; forefathers of American special forces

soil for almost a decade. The British may have had a formidable army, but unconventional tactics rather than serried ranks of regiments were needed to fight the Native Americans on their own terrain. The Rangers were made up of American frontiersmen and backwoodsmen—including Native Americans—and Rogers incorporated their unparalleled hunting, tracking, stealth, and killing skills into his special tactics. They wore a green uniform better suited for covert work than the conventional—often bright red—dress of a British soldier.

To aid the training of new additions to the ranks of both the Rangers and the regular army, in 1757 Robert Rogers created a 28-point guideline for specialist tactics and unconventional warfare. They were his standing orders, known as the "Rules of Ranging" or "Rogers' Rules," which established the founding principles for American special forces, and particularly the 75th Regiment—the Rangers, in the 20th century. Lieutenant Colonel William Darby read the rules to the elite commandos of the 1st Rangers Battalion to inspire his men just before they entered the fray in World War II. Rule 2 gives an indication of their continued relevance: "Whenever you are ordered out to the enemy's forts or frontiers for discoveries, if your number be small, march in a single file, keeping at such a distance from each other as to prevent one shot from killing two men, sending one man, or more, forward, and the like on each side, at the distance of twenty yards from the main body, if the ground you march over will admit of it, to give the signal to the officer of the approach of an enemy." Such techniques are a matter of standard practice in today's special forces throughout the world, but in the mid-18th century they were a revelation and a sign of Rogers' military genius.

The initial Rangers unit consisted of little more than a few dozen men who took part in raids and reconnaissance missions into enemy territory along the northeast frontiers. Their unique ability to adapt to the difficult terrain

Above: Abenaki Indians, whose village was hit by a long-range surprise attack by Rogers' Rangers in 1759

Above: Robert Rogers, deemed by many to be the father of US Special Forces, changed sides and supported the British in the American Revolutionary War

Opposite: Made up of frontiersmen, backwoodsmen and Native Americans, Rogers' Rangers continually adapted to harsh terrain and wore snowshoes in battle in 1758–8

was soon on display in what became known as the First Battle on Snowshoes in January 1751. Rogers' band of 74 men captured seven French soldiers at Lake Champlain in upstate New York, but they were then met by a force of about 180 Frenchmen, French-Canadians and Indians. The outnumbered Rangers had the advantage of wearing snowshoes, while, as later described by the admiral and explorer Louis Antoine de Bougainville, the French were "floundering in snow up to their knees." The Rangers lost 14 men and retreated, but not before they had inflicted 37 casualties on the French.

The Second Battle on Snowshoes commenced on 13 March the following year, when the Rangers laid a trap for what appeared to be an enemy patrol of around a hundred men near the French stronghold of Fort St. Frédéric in the same region. The initial ambush proved to be a success, but the French patrol was soon followed by a much larger force, vastly outnumbering Rogers' band of Rangers and regulars. Rogers would later claim that his men killed about 100 French and Indians, and wounded about the same number, but his troops also incurred heavy losses, with 125 killed. The French reported that Rogers himself had been slain, but he escaped, according to legend, by sliding down a sheer mountainside for 400 feet to land on the frozen surface of Lake George. The rock-face is still known as "Rogers' Slide."

Officers of the conventional British army had been at odds with the Rangers unit almost since its inception, appalled by these unorthodox and free-spirited Americans. In December 1757, some of the Rangers revolted in the Whipping Post Mutiny, after British soldiers had whipped two members of the Rangers. It was only after Rogers himself intervened that the mutiny was calmed.

The British admired the work of the American unit, but wanted to replace it, or at least dilute it, with their own, more loyal, and disciplined soldiers. They also wanted to match the French territorial advantage of working with

Native Americans who knew how to fight in mountainous and rugged terrain. By 1758, the number of soldiers described as Rangers had expanded to over a thousand men, including British and Indian companies, but Rogers' American unit remained his own personal force, often augmented by Stockbridge Indians and British regulars.

Rogers' Rangers continued reconnaissance, raiding and patrolling missions in the Lake George area, and took part in skirmishes and battles that enabled the British to capture Fort Carillon in 1759. Later that year, in October, the American Rangers conducted the St. Francis Raid on an Abenaki village in the French Province of Canada. St. Francis had become a centre from which the Native Americans raided British colonial holdings, so a covert mission

into enemy territory to wipe it out was deemed highly important. The Rangers acted as instructed, undertaking a lengthy journey, wading through miles of boggy land, sneaking into the area, and then using rafts to finally reach their destination. All the while, French and Indian forces, who knew an enemy unit was in the area, tried and failed to track them down.

The Rangers took the village in a surprise attack at dawn, torched it and slaughtered up to 300 of the inhabitants—including women and children—in what is deemed one of the least noble episodes in colonial history. In his journal, Robert Kirkwood, a Scottish soldier who would later fight for the Continental Army in the American Revolutionary War, noted, "This was, I believe, the bloodiest scene in all America, our revenge being complete."

The Rangers lost only one man, with seven wounded, but their problems had only just begun. Deep in enemy territory and attempting to traverse 200 miles of uncharted terrain at speed, while encumbered by prisoners, they were hunted and harried by French and Indian forces. They were desperately short of rations, so Rogers broke up the force into bands of about a dozen men so that they could hunt and forage for their own food more adequately. The units would find it harder to defend themselves, but at least they might not starve to death. Up to 50 of them would eventually be killed or captured by the 700-strong French-Indian force that had been sent after them. It was

Opposite: George Washington feared Rogers was a spy and rejected his services at the beginning of the American Revolutionary War

THE FIRST RANGER UNITS

ROGERS' RANGERS WERE predated by the Rangers of Benjamin Church. He created an elite unit in the mid-1670s during King Philip's War, waged by the English and Native American allies against Metacomet (otherwise known as King Philip) and a coalition of New England tribes. Church, a Puritan born in the Plymouth Colony, craftily asked Native American allies to teach his troops how to fight like them. His Rangers became an irregular fighting unit skilled at raiding and fighting in forests and swamps, leading to a successful English campaign. Rogers' Rangers were also immediately predated by Gorham's Rangers, recruited in 1744. Made up of Native Americans led by British officers, they specialized in amphibious raids and guerilla warfare in Nova Scotia. Rogers' Rangers, however, became the historical model for the American special forces, not least because of the 28 "Rules of Ranging," which are followed to this day.

reported that some of the captured were taken back to St. Francis, the village they had so brutally raided, to be killed by grieving Abenaki women.

Roger wrote that the Rangers faced "many days' tedious march over steep rocky mountains or thro' wet dirty swamps, with the terrible attendants of fatigue and hunger." There are reports of the Rangers suffering from exposure and eating roots, bark, insects, mushrooms, and rotting flesh. One soldier reported that they were forced to "eat our shoes and belts, and broil our powder horns." There was also a much darker secret to the survival of the Rangers. Kirkwood claimed that Rogers killed an Indian woman prisoner, and the troops butchered and ate her, and there are other similar reports of the cannibalism of the desperate Rangers.

After nine days of hardship, Rogers' troops reached an agreed rendezvous point where they had arranged to pick up supplies for the remainder of the journey back to safety. But there was nothing there. In desperation, Rogers took

Below: Following the Raid on St Francis, Rogers' men found that their support team had already left the rendezvous point, leaving them stranded in enemy territory without supplies

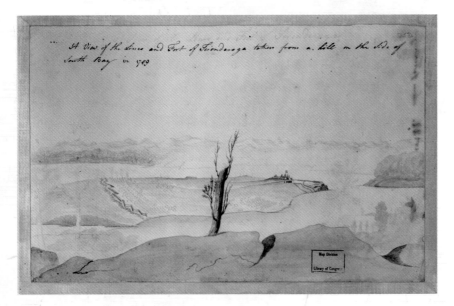

A view of the lines and Fort of Ticonderoga taken from a hill on the Side of South Bay in 1759

Left: Fort Carillon (later renamed Fort Ticonderoga), seen in the distance, was taken from the French with the aid of Rogers' Rangers. The text on the picture reads "A view of the lines and Fort of Ticonderoga taken from the hill on the side of South Bay in 1759."

three soldiers, left the rest of his starving men and said he would return in ten days. They built rafts and drifted down the Connecticut River to reach the Fort at Number 4, the northernmost British settlement in New Hampshire. His condition on arrival was described as being so weak he could barely walk, but he returned to his men on the tenth day, with supplies, as promised. Against the odds, two-thirds of Rogers' men survived the return expedition, and their survival skills would become legendary amongst later special forces.

Rogers' Rangers would earn further accolades for their part in the capture of Fort Detroit in 1760 and for their actions in suppressing Pontiac's Rebellion in 1763, but with the end of French and Indian War, their role as a standing unit had passed.

At the start of the American Revolutionary War, Rogers preferred to join the Patriots, as did many of the Rangers, rather than work for his previous employers, but George Washington rejected his services. The commander of the Patriots feared that Rogers was a spy. Perhaps he was right to question Rogers' true loyalty to the cause of independence: soon after his rejection, Rogers raised a new Loyalist battalion, the Queen's Rangers, to fight against the Patriots. According to the contemporary account of Consider Tiffany, Rogers even played a duplicitous role in the capture of the great American hero and spy, Nathan Hale. Whatever Rogers' true allegiances, his elite unit had created a blueprint for future special forces.

Imperial Guard

Napoleon's personal reserve force which was feared across Europe as the French dictator expanded his empire

"THE GUARD DIES, it does not surrender," General Pierre Cambronne shouted at the approaching enemy troops. The French army was in tatters, the bodies of colleagues lay mangled, strewn, and lifeless on the battlefield of Waterloo, Napoleon had fled, and the Imperial Guard was surrounded, but still the Guardsmen refused to give up their arms. According to legend, Cambronne himself did not share their sentiment. His next words were, "Cambronne surrenders, he does not die."

It was 18 June 1815. The Imperial Guard had gained a fearsome reputation, having been created by Napoleon Bonaparte just 11 years earlier. They had proved to be a courageous and loyal *corps d'élite*, notching up notable successes on behalf of the French emperor who was determined to have all of Europe at his mercy.

The origin of the unit was the Consular Guard formed in 1800 with just 2,000 men, many of whom had been loyal to Napoleon in his coup in 1799. They had been soldiers in the Guards of the Directory and Legislature Corps who supported the general when he swept to power as the First Consul of France and ended the French

FACT FILE

REGION: Europe
ERA: 1804-15
KEY ENCOUNTERS: Battle of Eylau 1807; Battle of Wagram 1809; Battle of Waterloo 1815
TACTICS AND TECHNIQUES: Cavalry and infantry used as reserves to enact a *coup de grâce* in battle and protect Napoleon
WEAPONRY: Lance; saber; musket; artillery
LEGACY: An elite force that helped Napoleon ravage Europe

Left: Napoleon Crossing the Alps by Jacques-Louis David, depicting Napoleon's journey before the Battle of Marengo in 1800. The artist painted five versions of the portrait between 1801 and 1805

revolutionary era. The infantry consisted of two companies of *Chasseurs à pied* (light infantry used for rapid action) and one of *Grenadiers* (heavier infantry), supported by two companies of cavalry and one of artillery.

Once he had assumed power, Napoleon soon began to assert his imperial ambitions. The Consular Guard proved itself fighting the Austrians at the Battle of Marengo in June 1800 and was soon expanded to four infantry battalions, with an enlarged cavalry including a squadron of Mamluks gained from Napoleon's campaign in Egypt. When Napoleon ceased to pretend that he was not a dictator and took the title of Emperor in 1804, the unit became the Imperial Guard. It is a testament to the size of his ambition that the Imperial Guard numbered over 50,000 less than a decade later.

The Guard was already on its way to becoming an elite before it took the imperial moniker. Its soldiers were some of the best and most experienced in the whole of Europe. They received a higher wage than the rest of the troops, they formed Napoleon's palace guard, and the officers were a privileged echelon within both the military and social hierarchy. Such a garlanded position belied the fact that Guards were gruff, gnarly veterans with a huge capacity for alcohol, even while on campaign. Jean Barres, a

Right: Statue of a soldier of the Imperial Guard, whom Napoleon trusted with his life and affectionately nicknamed "the Grumblers"

new recruit to the Chasseurs, reported in November 1805, "Despite the snow, which was falling in avalanches, the foragers ... found some excellent cellars of Hungarian wines ... A benevolent spectator of this gigantic orgy, drinking next to nothing, I marveled, without being dazzled, at the surprising capacity of some of the men, which was truly gargantuan."

Napoleon used the Guard as a pivotal strategic tool on the battlefield, and they would be renowned for their valor right up to the final moment of the final battle. Although inspiring jealousy in the rest of the army, they were referred to as "the Immortals," and the sight of them taking to the battlefield in their trademark bearskin hats inspired and motivated the regular French soldiers. Unlike elites such as the Praetorians, the Janissaries, and the Streltsy, the Guard did not survive long enough to become a bloated, disloyal anachronism, feeding off its own power.

Also unlike other elites, the expansion of the Guard did not mean that its quality became greatly diluted. Napoleon, who for all his faults as an ambitious power-monger had an exceptionally astute military mind, personally inspected the application of every volunteer, making sure that each one had the right military acumen to become a member of his elite force. His interest in every detail of the Guard, and his regard for its skill and loyalty, never waned during his dictatorship.

The original veterans of the Imperial Guard became known as the Old Guard—whom Napoleon would refer to with some fondness as "the Grumblers" due to their insatiable appetite for moaning about all aspects of military life. The names of the Middle Guard, established during Napoleon's war against Prussia in 1806, and the Young Guard, recruited from 1809 onwards from the best conscripts in the army's regular battalions, reflected their later addition to the Imperial Guard, although they also included experienced and hardy veterans. As well as the Mamluk cavalry, the Imperial Guard was enforced by other foreign elites, with regiments of lancers made up of Polish, Dutch, and Lithuanian units.

In tactical terms, it was the cavalry of the Imperial Guard to whom Napoleon would most often turn, as he often left the Imperial infantry in reserve for a *coup de grâce* at a pivotal point in battle. In one of Napoleon's most acclaimed victories, the Battle of Austerlitz on 2 December 1805, it was left to the Guard's cavalry to mount an impressive defense against the counterattacking charge of the Russian Imperial cavalry. For this courageous

effort Napoleon awarded his Guard the title "The Invincibles." Once the Russian charge had been repulsed, victory for the French was assured.

Two years later, the Old Guard would play an important role in the less conclusive Battle of Eylau. The Guard had helped repel the forces of the Russians, but on the second day of battle the Russians had fought back so hard that the centre of the French formation was broken and even Napoleon's command headquarters were under threat. Battalions of the Old Guard counterattacked with a bayonet charge that completely decimated the advancing Russian column. The decisive move enabled Joachim Murat to mount one of the most impressive cavalry charges in history: the 11,000-strong mounted force of Napoleon's Grande Armée ran straight through the Russian infantry and then divided in two so that Murat could wheel into the enemy cavalry. The Guard's cavalry followed through with a secondary assault. Murat's main cavalry units then re-formed and mounted another charge, before the Guard covered its retreat. The charges had caused carnage.

The result was a draw, with about 20,000 casualties on each side, leading the French general, Marshal Ney, to succinctly summarize the scene with the words, "What a massacre! And without result." If it hadn't been for the Guard and Murat's cavalry, however, Napoleon's army would have been slaughtered, and the Emperor himself would have fallen. Even though he had faced annihilation, the little dictator had once again proved his worth as a military logician: the rapid cavalry assault had only been made possible by his decision to replace Murat's horses with far superior beasts he had requisitioned in Prussia; and his tactic of keeping the elite Old Guard in reserve had saved both the battle, and his life.

Opposite: Portrait of Napoleon by Andrea Appiani (1805)

THE GRENADIER GUARDS

AN ELITE FORCE of the British army, the Grenadier Guards were named after their brave exploits against the French Imperial Guard at the Battle of Waterloo in 1815. Previously known as the 1st Regiment of Foot Guards, they showed great valor and marksmanship as they mounted the volley-fire defense of their position against the assault of the Imperial Guard, and then broke them with a bayonet charge. They were consequently named after their elite counterparts, the esteemed Grenadiers of the Imperial Guard, and adopted their bearskin headwear, which they continue to wear. However, it turned out that the Grenadiers were named after the wrong regiment as they had actually fought the Chasseurs.

Right: The Battle of Ligny, 1815, a great but final victory for the Imperial Guard

Below: First Consul Bonaparte by Antoine-Jean Gros (1802); Napoleon would create the elite Imperial Guard as soon as he became Emperor

The Young Guard came to greater prominence in the Battle of Aspern-Essling against a superior Austrian force in May 1809, but the battle marked Napoleon's first defeat in his multi-fronted assault on the established powers of Europe. Pride was restored less than two months later in the Battle of Wagram, which, with 300,000 combatants, was the biggest battle that had ever been fought on European soil. The Imperial cavalry again proved its worth in a decisive victory.

Napoleon was forced to abdicate in 1814 after his Grande Armée had been destroyed in Russia, and he went into exile. Before he left, he delivered a personal speech to his Old Guard, saying: "For 20 years I have accompanied you on the path to honor and glory ... Farewell, my children ... Would that I could press you all to my heart."

He soon returned from exile and the Guard re-formed to face another onslaught from the allied powers of Europe. The Emperor's tactic of holding back the elite Old Guard proved vital again in the Battle of Ligny on 16 June 1815. The Prussians, who were themselves an excellent army, held firm at Saint-Amand against the Young Guard before the Middle Guard seized the initiative and took the town. However, the centre of the Prussian force remained impregnable at neighboring Ligny, so Napoleon played his hand and sent in the Old Guard. In the midst of thunder, lightning, and heavy rain, they attacked at speed and swept through the town. Fighting off the esteemed Prussian cavalry, they re-formed into a square, broke the resolve of the Prussians, and sent them into retreat. However, the Battle of Ligny would prove to be the final victory for Emperor Napoleon I and his Imperial Guard.

At the Battle of Waterloo, just two days later on 18 June 1815, the French faced the combined might of the Prussian and British armies. The Young Guard fought valiantly but the Middle Guard let Napoleon down. In a desperate move, he had sent them to attack the center of the Duke of Wellington's British army, but they were repulsed. As Marshal Ney reported, "this body of troops was too weak to resist, for a long time, the forces opposed to it by the enemy, and it was soon necessary to renounce the hope which this attack had, for a few moments, inspired." The Guard was already being decimated by regimented volley-fire when the British light infantry wheeled into their flank and charged. The Guard retreated without an official order for the first time in its history. When the rest of the French forces saw "the Immortals" fleeing, they knew the game was up.

The Old Guard, as usual, stepped in to save their leader, who was at his command post in a town square. As the majority of the French army fled around them in scenes of carnage, the Guard held its formation and covered the retreat in the face of a bombardment of artillery fire and cavalry charges. Ney reported: "These brave grenadiers, the choice of the army, forced successively to retire, yielded ground foot by foot, till, overwhelmed by numbers, they were almost entirely annihilated." As Cambronne allegedly shouted at the enemy in the final throes of the battle, the Guard "does not surrender." The Grumblers remained a devoted elite until the very final hour and preferred to die. After the disastrous battle, their defeated Emperor abdicated.

French Foreign Legion

The hardened foreign soldiers of the French army, famous for their psychological and physical toughness

ON THE ONE HAND, the soldiers of the French Foreign Legion are regarded as the world's most highly trained corps of mercenaries. On the other, they are a rabble of ruthless criminals, madmen, and misfits barely controlled by extreme discipline—their reputation is such that when Spain decided to copy the Legion, one opponent called it "The misbegotten child of an unbalanced mind."

The romantic legacy of the French Foreign Legion is, of course, that its members are both elite soldiers and also troubled souls, hiding from their pasts. At its inception in 1831, it seemed highly unlikely that the *Légion étrangère* would become an elite force respected and feared throughout the world. France, and particularly Paris, had become the destination of choice for failed foreign revolutionaries who had either fled or become exiled from their own countries. The city was also teeming with unruly veterans of the disbanded German and Swiss mercenary regiments of the Bourbon monarchy, which had been ousted from power just a year earlier. Furthermore, there were plenty of

FACT FILE

REGION: Europe, North Africa, Far East

ERA: 1831–present day

KEY ENCOUNTERS: Battle of Camerone 1863; Battle of Bir-Hakeim 1942, Battle of Dien Bien Phu 1954; Kolwezi Operation 1978

TACTICS AND TECHNIQUES: Overseas force with tough physical training used in difficult terrain

WEAPONRY: FAMAS assault rifle; Spectra ballistic helmet

LEGACY: Brave foreign volunteers known for high endurance capabilities and *esprit de corps*

other troublesome individuals, both of French nationality and from other countries, that the new regime wanted removed from the city streets.

This unlikely collection of undesirables, including murderers and thieves, was recruited into the Foreign Legion, whose ordinance stipulated that the force could only serve outside France: no one wanted them to be trusted with arms within its borders. Part of the Legion's allure, which fuelled future legends, was its policy of *anonymat*: the volunteers did not have to provide any means of identification and had to use an assumed name. In one fell swoop, a man could wipe out his past. The Legion offered a life of adventure unburdened by the consequences of previous actions. Although officially recruits could not be French citizens, one of the Legion's secrets is that it has never been entirely "foreign." The rules of anonymity favored Frenchmen willing to escape from their lives, who often signed up as Swiss or Belgian.

Below: Modern-day French Legionnaires in their distinctive white kepis

The new Foreign Legion was promptly sent to Algeria, France's troublesome colony in North Africa. The force was originally split into battalions according to nationality: Germans, Swiss, Spanish, Italian, Polish, and Dutch-Belgian. Foreigners from less well-represented countries, such as England, which had 10 legionnaires in 1832, were spread amongst these battalions. The legionnaires were treated as an unwanted burden by the military establishment, who would send them to far, inhospitable outposts to pacify the locals. They were used in North Africa alongside another new unit of reprobates, the Battalions of Light Infantry of Africa, comprising criminals completing their military service and soldiers with terrible disciplinary records.

The dispensability of the Legion was made clear in 1835 when the French government simply handed it over to the Spanish to play a role in the First Carlist War. In an effort to make the force a proper unit rather than a collection of mutually antagonistic cliques, the national battalions were disbanded in favor of mixed ones. However, the numbers dropped so that by the end of 1838 there were only 500 legionnaires and the Legion was temporarily dissolved.

Below: The Foreign Legion parades through Roman ruins at Lambaesis during the Algerian War in 1958

Above: The Battle of Camerone, 1863, in which six remaining legionnaires mounted a bayonet charge against a huge Mexican force

It was hardly an auspicious beginning for the corps, but certain principles that would form its core and enhance its reputation had already been established. Due to the nature of the unit, harsh discipline was deemed essential; so was unconventional training, as the men had to survive in the extremely harsh terrain of North Africa, suffering the desert climate of extreme heat and cold, with little possibility of food or water to augment their rations. These tough conditions and the abandonment of the national battalions started to create an *esprit de corps* that would become the hallmark of the Legion.

To this day, Article 2 of the Legion's Code of Honor, which every trainee must know by heart, is: "Each legionnaire is your brother in arms whatever his nationality, his race or his religion might be. You show him the same close solidarity that links the members of the same family." The legionnaires may fight for France, but above all, they fight for each other: their motto is "The Legion is Our Fatherland."

A new Foreign Legion regiment was soon formed and would begin to establish its military reputation in the Crimean War, playing an essential

Above and opposite:
The slow march of the Foreign Legion, with precisely 88 steps per minute, has become a signature of their public displays

part in the Siege of Sebastopol in 1855, followed by the campaign in Italy in 1859, where the French General, Patrice Mac-Mahon, was so sure of its skills that he exclaimed, "Here is the Legion! It's in the bag," prior to their victory at Magenta.

Another article of the Legion's Code of Honor states, "In combat, you act without passion and without hate, you respect defeated enemies, and you never abandon your dead, your wounded or your arms." The courageousness of the Legionnaires and unwillingness to surrender came to the fore in Mexico in 1863 at the Battle of Camerone. A company of just 65 men was attacked by a force of 2,000 Mexicans and defended itself in a hacienda. Almost all the soldiers were killed in intensive fire, and the remaining six had run out of ammunition. Instead of surrendering, the six men mounted a bayonet charge against the huge force. Three of them were killed and three wounded; out of respect the Mexican general allowed the three survivors to accompany the body of their dead captain back to France.

Despite its enduring reputation as an anonymous, garrulous, disloyal—but well-trained—band of foreign misfits and cut-throats, the Legion proved that it could be trusted with the protection of the French nation on French soil. France was running out of troops in the 1870-1871 war with the Prussians, and Paris itself was under siege in 1870, so the rule against the Legion fighting in France had to be broken. Despite a strong contingent of legionnaires originating from Prussia, the Legion remained loyal to its principles and succeeded in retaking Orléans. Although they could not save Paris, the legionnaires served with distinction.

They soon returned, however, to far-off lands to help France pursue its international interests. The Legion undertook campaigns in Vietnam and Madagascar, but its main role continued to be the attempted colonization of northern and western Africa, with attempts to pacify Algeria, Morocco, Benin, Sudan and the Ivory Coast, where its specialist skills, training and discipline came to the fore.

It would return to France in World War I, and again enhance its reputation as an elite force. Many foreign nationals, especially Americans prior to the US entering the fray, signed up as legionnaires, and there was initially conflict between the fresh-faced, politically idealistic volunteers and the battle-hardened, elite veterans, which was not helped by the chaos of the French campaign as the destruction raged around them. Despite this, the Legion fought with valor on the Western and Macedonian fronts. Its 3rd Regiment became one of the most decorated units in the entire French army.

Right: A legionnaire in Indochina 1954

Between the wars, the Legion, which now had 30,000 soldiers, continued to be based at headquarters at Sidi-bel-Abbès in Algeria and conducted further campaigns in Morocco and Syria.

By the start of World War II, the Legion's famous uniform of a white kepi with neck cover, blue sash, and red and green epaulettes was established. In order to reinforce the *esprit de corps*, regimental rituals with an emphasis on history were also adopted. The Legion's exploits at Camerone are still commemorated on its feast day and its flag. The Legion's music, "Le Boudin" ("the blood sausage," possibly named after the rolled blanket that formed part of the legionnaire's equipment), had already been in use for decades, but over time the Legion's slow march to the tune −88 steps per minute— would become one of its distinctive traditions.

At the outbreak of World War II, volunteers again flooded the ranks of the Foreign Legion in the fight against Germany. In particular, Jews from central Europe and Republicans defeated by Franco in the Spanish Civil War bolstered the numbers. The Legion was split in two as some supported the German puppet government of Vichy France, while others joined General Charles de Gaulle and the cause of the Free French. Legionnaire fought legionnaire in the Middle East in 1941, but many Vichy legionnaires later defected to the Allies.

The Legion also fought in Norway and, of course, North Africa, where its guerrilla-warfare experience was essential. At the Battle of Bir-Hakeim in Libya, 1942, the Free French, led by the Legion, were alone in withstanding the might of Rommel's German and Italian force as it swept through North Africa. Trapped in a fort with limited food and water, and facing bombardment from both land and air, the legionnaires held out for day after day until the British could organize their retreat. Winston Churchill would applaud the defense of the fort: "Holding back for fifteen days Rommel's offensive, the free French of Bir-Hakeim had contributed to save Egypt and

KOLWEZI RESCUE OPERATION

ON 11 MAY 1978, 4,000 Front for the National Liberation of the Congo (FNLC) rebels swarmed into Kolwezi in Zaire and took 3,000 Europeans hostage. The Europeans were mainly mining engineers and their families working in the mineral-rich region. On 16 May, Zairean paratroopers attempted a disastrous assault, which only managed to provoke the FNLC into killing hostages. Zaire called for French and Belgian assistance, and by 19 May the 2nd Foreign Parachute Regiment of the Legion was in Zaire, ready and prepared. A 450-man unit dropped, in daylight, from just 820 feet into the open-air hippodrome in the city while under enemy fire. Six men were wounded while another who missed the drop zone was hacked to death in the street. The legionnaires used their sniping and street-fighting skills to dismantle enemy positions, and knocked out an armored vehicle with an 89 mm anti-tank rocket launcher. Within three hours, they had secured most of Kolwezi and then ambushed a rebel attempt to counterattack. Reinforced by a second parachute drop, within two days the legionnaires had control of the entire city and released 2,800 Europeans at the cost of a handful of men.

Above: The motto of the legionnaires, famous for their loyalty to each other, is "The Legion is Our Fatherland"

the Suez Canal's destinies." The delay effected by the Legion enabled the Allies to reorganize its forces, rand prepare them for Al-Alamein.

At the end of World War II, the German component of the Foreign Legion became more significant as the defeated German army was disbanded and its soldiers sought to continue their military careers. Secretly, members of the notorious Waffen SS joined the Legion's numbers, although the French intelligence service ensured that anyone accused of war crimes was refused. The percentage of Germans in the unit may have been as high as 40 percent when the Legion was immediately called into action again, this time in Indochina.

The Foreign Legion had become a household name across the world before the war, thanks to the authors and filmmakers who were attracted to the romanticism of these unknown men with dubious pasts fighting with such discipline and courage in tough terrain. For the rest of the 20th century, Englishmen such as Simon Murray, who signed up as a lovesick 19-year-old public schoolboy in the 1960s, were inspired to join by *Beau Geste*, an adventure novel by Percival Christopher Wren, published in 1924 and adapted for the screen several times. Murray soon found that life in the Legion was no motion picture: he had enlisted for a minimum of five years of brutal training, harsh discipline, and danger in an oppressive martial world enthused by the ethic, "March or die."

In the immediate postwar era, the Legion started to adopt the skills of a modern-day special force. The 2nd Foreign Parachute Battalion, which Murray was to join, was founded in 1948 and was thrown into the Indochina campaign. In 1954, paratroopers were dropped into the Indochina war zone to reinforce other legionnaires at the Battle of Dien Bien Phu, but the operation was a heroic disaster. The French headquarters were surrounded, with the radio operator sending a final message: "The enemy has overrun us. We are blowing up everything. Vive la France!" The legionnaires, in the noble spirit of Camerone, refused to surrender and attempted a breakout. No one escaped and the prisoners had to endure years of hardship in the POW camps of the Viet Minh.

The 2nd Foreign Parachute Battalion was upgraded to regiment status a year later, and has taken part in campaigns and operations in Algeria, Chad, Zaire, the Gulf War, and, most recently, Afghanistan and Mali. It has become the lead unit of the French rapid reaction force, trained for special operations in enemy territory. The unit is made up of the best recruits in the French army, but it also takes any who can endure intense physical training and psychological tests in difficult terrain and extreme weather. Candidates then undergo parachuting, weaponry, and hand-to-hand combat training. The old legionnaire qualities of high discipline, strong survival skills, ability to fight in challenging terrain, and solid *esprit de corps* continue into the modern era of high-tech weaponry and equipment.

The 1st Foreign Parachute Regiment did not serve with such distinction. In terms of loyalty, they provided the Legion's darkest hour in 1961 when the whole regiment rebelled against President Charles de Gaulle's deal to end the war against Algeria and give the country its independence. They joined the "Secret Armed Organization" and attempted a coup in Algiers. After the coup failed, the regiment was disbanded.

In 1962, the Legion left its base in Algeria and is now quartered mainly in France and Corsica. Anonymity remains assured, but thorough background checks are made by Interpol and, since 2010, soldiers have been allowed to serve under their own name.

British Commandos

The UK's amphibious raiding force, known for extreme physical fitness and tactical agility

"IT WAS PRETTY CLEAR that we were going to take casualties—the risks were tremendous," Corran Purdon recalled in conversation with the journalist and former soldier Sean Rayment in *Tales from the Special Forces Club*. "I think we all knew a lot of us would not be coming back." Purdon was describing a real-life Mission Impossible: the Commando raid on the docks of St. Nazaire in 1942. Purdon didn't mind the risk. He was a natural-born Commando and, despite the odds, he didn't for one moment think this mission would fail: "I never doubted that it would be a success."

The Commandos had been formed in 1940, in the words of British Prime Minister Winston Churchill, as "specially trained troops of the hunter class, who can develop a reign of terror down the enemy coast." They would specialize in covert, amphibious raids into enemy territory in a strategy called "butcher and bolt," causing mayhem and destruction before quickly slipping away into the night. Purdon, an eager soldier in the Royal Ulster Rifles, facing too long sitting on the sidelines in the midst of World War II, said, "I wanted to be part of that."

FACT FILE

REGION: Europe, North Africa, Middle East, Far East

ERA: 1940–present day

KEY ENCOUNTERS: St. Nazaire Raid 1942; D-Day Landings 1944; Falklands War 1982; Operation Telic 2003; Operation Herrick 2006

TACTICS AND TECHNIQUES: Covert amphibious and airborne raids into enemy territory, using sabotage techniques

WEAPONRY: Fairbairn-Sykes Fighting Knife; SA80 A2 assault rifle; light machine gun; 9 mm pistol; mortars

LEGACY: One of the world's most highly trained amphibious assault elites

The tough, rigorous and unconventional training he underwent still forms the basis of Royal Marine Commando training today. Rather than endless drills and disciplined marching, they practiced moving at speed, with heavy loads, over difficult terrain and across dangerous waters. Assault courses, river crossings, rock-climbing, extreme physical training, and speed marches covering 15 miles in just three hours, while carrying 60 lb packs plus equipment, were the order of the day.

They became excellent marksmen on the range but were also trained to shoot a heavy Bren gun from the hip while on the move, and a powerful anti-tank gun while standing up, which would knock most men over. All men

Above: The modern Royal Marine Commandos combine rigorous training and expert specialist skills to make them one of the most respected forces in the world

were equipped with a double-bladed fighting knife, which they would strap to their calves for covert operations. Armed combat exercises would be conducted under live fire, often at night, and the Commandos were also highly proficient at unarmed, hand-to-hand fighting. Demolition was a significant element of the training for some officers, as the Commandos would be used in covert operations to knock out German ships and blow up ports.

The original Commandos were made up of infantrymen who had signed up as "volunteers wanted for hazardous service." And hazardous service was exactly what the force got in Operation Chariot, the raid on St. Nazaire.

The Germans had built a massive new battleship, the *Tirpitz*, which was a deadly threat to the merchant convoys running vital food supplies to Britain across the North Atlantic. However, the British saw a weakness in the size of this new super-ship: the only dry dock on the Atlantic coast large enough to house the *Tirpitz* for running repairs was St. Nazaire on the Normandy shore of German-occupied France. If the dry dock

Top: Commandos relaxing after conducting a covert, night-time raid in 1943

Above: Commandos moving inland from Sword Beach, Normandy, on D-Day, 6 June 1944

was knocked out, the Germans would not dare risk deploying the *Tirpitz* in the North Atlantic. Without a port for repairs, the *Tirpitz* would struggle to get home to Germany if it was damaged in an engagement. The mission was vital to British fortunes in the Battle of the North Atlantic.

The plan was simple. British Commandos would load an old US destroyer, rechristened the HMS *Campbeltown*, with four tons of explosives and sail it six miles from the mouth of the Loire estuary to the St. Nazaire dock, in the company of a flotilla of 16 motor launches containing Commandos. Once there, the *Campbeltown* would be rammed into the dock gates, and the 622 Commandos would destroy the significant port facilities, U-boats, and their defenses. Shortly before the high explosives on the *Campbeltown* were detonated, blowing up the docks, the Commandos would escape back to the Atlantic in their motor boats.

The plan may have been simple, but it was also extraordinarily foolhardy. Because of its military importance, the inlet of the Loire running from the Atlantic to the docks was intensely defended by 5,000 German troops, with dozens of fortified gun emplacements on both banks and around the docks. The *Campbeltown* and the motor launches would be exposed on the water and beset by intense fire all along the estuary. There was even a chance that the *Campbeltown* would explode before it reached its destination, killing all the Commandos and Royal Navy crew on board. The men in the motor launches were no safer: the wooden boats were unarmored and, because of the distance needed to be covered in the operation, they were also heavily loaded with fuel. It would take only one accurate projectile to blow a motor

THE FIRST BRITISH COMMANDOS

THE WORD "COMMANDO" comes from the kommando fighters of South Africa. In Afrikaans, a *kommando* (deriving from the Portuguese *"comando"*) refers to the "mobile infantry unit" in which citizens were temporarily commanded to fight. The British picked up the word during the Second Boer War in 1899–1902, but typical commando activity had been practiced by the British for centuries, in the form of boarding-party raids on ships and assaults on ports. An island nation with a global empire, the British had a particular need for men who could fight on both sea and land. The Royal Navy organized special units for these activities in 1664 while fighting the Dutch. These skirmishers, saboteurs, and reconnaissance experts were designated the Royal Marine Light Infantry in 1855, which became a well-trained, highly mobile elite. In World War I, these Marines came into their own, leading the way at Gallipoli in 1915 and conducting the Zeebrugge Raid against the German U-boat port in 1918. These direct ancestors to the Commandos also fought as foot soldiers in the trenches of the Western Front. Their evolution into the Commandos of World War II was a natural transition: they had been pursuing special forces tactics for years.

launch, and its 15-man crew, sky high. Even if they managed to make it to St. Nazaire, there was little chance the Commandos would make it back. Operation Sitting Duck, rather than Operation Chariot, would have been a more accurate title.

Lord Mountbatten, the overseer of Commando operations, personally planned the assault. He was so aware of the dangers that he ensured that a note was read out excusing any man who did not want to go on the raid. According to Purdon, one tough captain stepped forward and handed a note of his own to the Commando colonel, saying, "Please may I withdraw?" The colonel was surprised, but then the captain and the men burst out laughing as it was just a prank—no one was backing down. The Commandos were trained and ready for their mission, whatever the cost. Once the operation began, Purdon recalled, "There was a great sense of euphoria on board. We were finally going to take part in a raid—that is why we became Commandos."

Amazingly, in the early hours of 28 March 1942, thanks to the simple deceit of flying a Nazi flag, the *Campbeltown* managed to sail down the estuary past the first few gun emplacements without engaging enemy fire. When the convoy was challenged and firing finally did begin, the signalman took advantage of the fact that British intelligence had cracked German naval codes and sent a message in German-style encoded Morse stating that the *Campbeltown* was a damaged German ship limping into port. This kept enemy fire off the Commandos for just a little while longer, but when it finally came it was a deadly barrage of crossfire from both banks. Purdon was on board the ship with his detonation crew while "shells were slamming into the side, and suddenly I saw a red-hot glowing shell puncture the wardroom ... we were bloody lucky it didn't explode."

More shells hit the *Campbeltown* full-on. Commandos on the decks were raked by machine-gun fire and motor launches exploded in flames, but the ship kept up its speed and successfully rammed straight into the dock gates. The Commandos kicked into action, spilling from the ship and the launches onto the docks, and mounting an assault on key positions, still under heavy bombardment. While other teams focused on the submarine pens, Purdon's personal target was a winding house used to winch ships into the docks. His team set their charges while under sporadic fire, pulled the ignition switches, and "watched the winding house jump about five feet in the air and then collapse." Other detonation teams had similar successes.

Most of the motor launches had been hit, at a great loss of life, and the Commandos' exit strategy dematerialized. The colonel calmly informed the remaining force that they were going to fight their way through the town, which was manned by a huge German force, and make their way to Spain—over 350 miles across enemy-occupied country without any rations. The resolve of the Commandos was already set in stone, even in those very early years. Purdon thought, "Okay, if that's the plan, we'd better get on with it."

Their "fire and movement" skills came in handy, running from shadow to shadow. They managed to cross a heavily defended bridge but Purdon was blown into the air by a hand grenade. Despite suffering injuries, he got back to his feet and fought through the streets, alleyways and gardens with his fellow

Above: Royal Marine Commandos traverse snow-covered mountains during the specialist "Himalayan Warrior" altitude training exercise in 2007

Above: Royal Marine Commandos on a training exercise

Opposite: Commandos on deployment in Jackal armored patrol vehicles in Afghanistan

Commandos. Their days were numbered though. Daylight was breaking and the depleted force took refuge in a cellar, where they were soon surrounded by Germans. In all, 105 members of the Royal Navy and 64 Commandos had been killed, and 215 were taken prisoner, including Purdon.

"Was it worth it?" Purdon must have thought to himself, facing the prospect of years as a prisoner of war. It was. A few minutes later, he heard the *Campbeltown* explode.

The Commandos had taken part in one of the most impossible missions of World War II, and despite the number of dead, wounded and captured, they had succeeded. St. Nazaire was destroyed and played no further part in the war. The feared *Tirpitz* was never able to join the Battle of the Atlantic, and the Allies gained the upper hand in the ocean. Not only was Operation Chariot a strategic success, it was a tremendous morale booster on the home front.

Meanwhile, Corran Purdon would attempt to escape from POW camps so many times that he ended up in the brutal Colditz camp for the rest of the war. When he was finally released by US troops, he secretly joined their

Above: Modern Commandos are trained to face extreme fighting conditions anywhere in the world

ranks and continued fighting against the Germans. On his return to Britain, Purdon was awarded the Military Cross. Five other men received the Victoria Cross for their exploits in Operation Chariot and many more were awarded other medals or mentioned in dispatches. The Commandos had established themselves as a highly skilled and courageous elite willing to fight against the odds, and win.

Prior to Operation Chariot, Commandos from the British Army and Royal Marines had already performed heroics in raids against Germany and her allies in Norway, where they sank eight enemy ships in a single raid, and they would be called upon to make landings under fire in the Italian campaign. At Dieppe in August 1942, shortly after the raid of St. Nazaire, a team of just

18 Commandos scaled cliffs and managed to stop Germany's most effective gun battery from mounting a barrage against an Allied landing.

As a response to the unique skills of the Commandos, Adolf Hitler issued the secret "Commando Order" stating, in contravention of the code of war, that all Commandos should be executed even if they attempted to surrender.

In 1943, the individual Commando units were formally united under the banner of the Special Services Brigade, which soon changed its name to 1st Commando Brigade, in preparation for D-Day, where they performed adroitly. With their highly-rated amphibious assault skills, they then formed an essential part of the assault on Germany, crossing the Rhine, Weser and Elbe rivers in the concluding phase of the Allied victory in Europe. They also helped defeat the Japanese in Burma at the Battle of Hill 170 in January 1945.

The Commandos inspired the modern-day elite special forces in Britain: the Special Air Service and the Parachute Regiment. The army Commando units were disbanded at the end of the war but the Royal Navy has maintained a Royal Marine Commando Brigade ever since.

Under the motto "By Sea, By Land," the Royal Marine Commandos became an elite force in their own right, continuing the tradition of tough physical training, specialist skills, and covert deployment established by those wartime Commandos.

The Marines' 3 Commando Brigade has been involved in every major British conflict since World War II. In the 1950s, the Commandos mounted an amphibious raid against Egyptian targets during the Suez Crisis, and achieved all their objectives in Operation Musketeer to take the canal. During this operation, they conducted what is believed to be the first ever helicopter-borne assault.

Along with two regiments of Paratroopers, 3 Commando Brigade spearheaded the successful demolition of Argentinian forces following the invasion of the Falklands in 1982, and saw further service in Operation Telic in Iraq, 2003, and Operation Herrick in Afghanistan, 2006. In Operation Telic, the Commandos returned to their roots to mount their first amphibious raid for two decades, taking the Al-Faw peninsula and the all-important naval port of Umm Qasr in a night operation. As a testament to the respect in which it is held worldwide, 3 Commando Brigade even commanded the US Marines in the operation. It remains one of the great elite units of modern warfare.

Waffen SS

The Aryan military force of the SS, which failed as an elite in World War II and was implicated in war crimes at the Nuremberg Trials

THE WAFFEN SHUTZSTAFFEN—the "armed protective squadron"—was created out of the personal bodyguard of Adolf Hitler, which was formed in 1925. After the close of World War II, the entire Waffen SS, with the exception of forced conscripts, was declared a criminal organization by the International Military Tribunal at the Nuremberg Trials and held responsible for war crimes and atrocities. It was regarded as an ideological and military elite that had worked hand-in-glove with Adolf Hitler in the pursuit of his extreme and inhuman policies.

In truth, by the end of the war, the Waffen SS was barely an elite in either military or ideological terms, and, in fact, many of the crimes for which it is sometimes held responsible were the work of its sister organization, the political body known as the Allgemeine SS. Nonetheless, some of its actions, not least the massacres at Malmedy in 1944, remain shockingly contrary to the accepted laws of war.

The personal bodyguard of Adolf Hitler was created in 1925, eight years before the Nazis came to power in Germany. In

FACT FILE

REGION: Europe

ERA: 1925–45

KEY ENCOUNTERS: Night of the Long Knives 1934; Battles of Kharkov and Kursk 1943; Invasion of Normandy 1944

TACTICS AND TECHNIQUES: Often used in specialist Panzer and motorcycle units and as an emergency reserve

WEAPONRY: Panzer, Jagdtiger, and Tiger armored vehicles; standard issue German army weapons

LEGACY: Accused of war crimes committed during World War II

an era of street violence mostly initiated by the Nazis themselves, Hitler needed to be protected from both political opponents and from the Nazi's own "street army," the notorious Sturmabteilung (SA) brown shirts of Ernst Röhm. The bodyguard, known as the Leibstandarte SS Adolf Hitler, included World War I veterans, but from the end of the 1920s the ranks were augmented by professionals from the middle classes who had lost their jobs during the Depression and had an ideological sympathy with Hitler's aspirations for the future of Germany. Soon, aristocrats were also counted amongst their number as they sought to recapture the glory days of Imperial Prussia. By the end of 1933, the tiny personal protection unit had grown to 50,000 men and, at the height of World War II, its descendant, the Waffen SS, numbered over 600,000 soldiers and 38 divisions.

Above: Heinrich Himmler, the leader of the SS, who introduced its legendary uniform

Heinrich Himmler, who joined the SS in 1925, became its leader, the Reichsführer in 1929. He wanted the SS to be a racially pure, ideological elite that would use extreme force to pursue Hitler's policies. Himmler was responsible for giving rise to the more bizarre, ritualistic elements of the SS, infusing it with special ceremonies, insignia, totems, and codes: he wanted to create a new order of quasi-religious knights in the manner of the Templars or, according to Hitler himself, the Jesuits. A significant motif of this new brotherhood was the SS uniform, which was black, in contrast to the SA's brown shirts. The SA were famous for their violence, debauchery, and immorality, and Himmler wanted the SS to be its opposite, purging any members, including drunkards, criminals, and homosexuals, who offended his skewed morality.

The SS's loyalty and its importance to Hitler's ambitions were proven at the end of June 1934. Having joined the government, Hitler used the SS to gain favor with the main German army and the conservative establishment by purging members of the paramilitary Nazi SA, as well as

innocent members of the public, in what became known as "The Night of the Long Knives." Ernst Röhm and more than 80 leading officers in the SA were killed by the SS. Hitler's actions opened the door to him becoming Germany's Chancellor. Following the dismantling of the SA, the SS stepped up from being a personal bodyguard to become a large political army, the SS Verfügungstruppe, becoming the Waffen SS in 1940 once the war had begun.

The SS was strongly linked to the Nazi ideals of racial purity, eugenic experiments, and selective breeding, and also to the aristocratic element left in the wake of the brutalism shown during the Night of the Long Knives. Selection came to be based on physical appearance, strength, and bearing. All recruits had to be over 5 feet 11 inches, and atheists were forbidden to join the ranks. The SS became an instrument of the Nazi theology of *Blut und Bloden* (blood and soil), which lauded pure-blooded German descent and the protection of the homeland; SS officers were required to prove they had 150 years of unsullied Aryan ancestry.

As war loomed, the SS was being prepared for the rigors of modern warfare. Rather than a traditional combination of artillery and infantry—the sort of formation that had dominated warfare strategy for centuries—the SS was supposed to become a close-knit elite corps that could be used unconventionally for infiltration into enemy territory and as shock troops. The highly regimented and hierarchical structure of the army and its training methods were seen as increasingly irrelevant. Instead of endless drills on the parade ground, sporting activity and a wide range of challenging physical exercises were given great emphasis. The purpose of the extremely intensive training regime was primarily physical fitness and small-arms proficiency, as well as ideological indoctrination.

Distinctions in rank were diluted, allowing the relations between the officers and the men to become more personal and even democratic, thereby creating a loyal brotherhood enthused by mutual respect rather than draconian discipline. The famous and rather casual SS salute, with the right forearm raised from the elbow, was adopted, and superiors, including Himmler, were just addressed by rank rather than as "Sir" ("*Herr*").

This Aryan brotherhood would be loyal to the principles of National Socialism, rather than the aims of the general German army or the public. However, in the huge and multifaceted conflict of World War II, the

Above: The famous all-black uniform of the Allgemeine SS (top) and the gray service uniform of the Waffen SS during World War II

THE MALMEDY MASSACRE

ONE CONVICTED WAFFEN SS war criminal was Joachim Peiper, an officer who had served as a personal adjutant to Himmler from 1938 to 1941 before progressing up the ranks to become a full colonel and lead his own Kampfgruppe Peiper of the Leibstandarte SS Adolf Hitler. He would become associated with the brutal execution of American prisoners of war and civilians in Belgium, December 1944. As his Panzer unit advanced during the Battle of the Bulge, his unit took US Army prisoners of war, and Peiper ordered their illegal execution. At his war trials, he defended himself and his soldiers while deferring responsibility: "I recognize that after the battles of Normandy my unit was composed mainly of young, fanatical soldiers. A good deal of them had lost their parents, their sisters, and brothers during the bombing. They had seen for themselves in Köln thousands of mangled corpses after a terror raid had passed. Their hatred for the enemy was such; I swear it and I could not always keep it under control." In one particular incident near Malmedy, he rounded up 120 American prisoners of war and shot them; some Waffen SS soldiers would later claim the Americans were trying to escape, but investigations revealed that many of them had been executed with a single bullet to the head or by blows from rifle butts. Even worse was to follow. More than 90 unarmed Belgian civilians, including women and children, were murdered at Stavelot. Other atrocities gave a total figure of more than 470 defenseless prisoners and civilians killed by Peiper's unit in the course of a couple of days. Peiper said: "My men are the products of total war, having grown up in the streets of scattered towns without any education. The only thing they knew was to handle weapons for the Reich. They were young people with a hot heart, and the desire to win or die." Peiper was sentenced to death, but he was let out of prison in 1956. He remained a devotee of Hitler long after the war had ceased, saying in 1967: "I was a Nazi and I remain one." In 1976, assassins believed to be former members of the French Resistance took their revenge and set his home alight. His burnt body was found with a gunshot wound to the chest.

Left: The scene after the horrific Malmedy Massacre, where the Waffen SS murdered 120 defenseless American prisoners of war in Belgium, December 1944

Above: A Panzer tank during World War II

Opposite: A recruiting poster for the Waffen SS

Waffen SS grew rapidly and unevenly, and few of its units reached the quality that Himmler and his senior officers expected from the force.

During the war the Waffen SS gave up the pretence of being the imagined Aryan elite: its racial purity became diluted as Scandinavians and even ethnic groups the Nazis had branded as "subhuman" joined its volunteer formations. Neither was it an impressive military elite, with only a few divisions—most notably some of the armored Panzer units—sustaining a level of military excellence in the field. By the close of World War II in 1945, in terms of both performance and tactical use in the field, most of the Waffen SS divisions were largely indistinguishable from the regular German Army. In fact, some were distinguishable only by their reputation for cruelty, not least the Dirlewanger Brigade, which was a penal unit led by a child rapist—hardly the moral elite envisaged by Himmler—while individual officers were responsible for the slaughtering of unarmed civilians and prisoners in a catalogue of wartime abuses.

Generally, the Waffen SS was not held in high regard by other elements of the army. Regular army officers pointed the finger at the ideological basis

Above: Himmler with the "Das Reich" SS Panzer division at Kharkov, 1943, where the Waffen SS served with distinction

for selection of SS officers as being responsible for unnecessary loss of life on the battlefield. The Desert Fox, Field Marshal Rommel, one of the great military strategists of World War II, did not want his son to join the SS as he distrusted and disliked Himmler, and did not regard him as an effective commanding officer.

During the war, Waffen SS soldiers were equipped with camouflaged helmet covers and smocks, but despite their supposedly elite status, most were given second-rate or captured weaponry and vehicles. However, there were some truly elite units within the Waffen SS, capable of scoring tactical successes. As well as the feared SS Panzer units, the SS motorcycle units were an effective specialist elite force. They rode BMW RW75s with MG34 machine gun-mounted sidecars. A battalion of motorcycle troops, composed of up to five companies of 18 motorcycles, would be attached to each Panzer division. They were used for reconnaissance or as shock troops during an assault on enemy positions.

The Waffen SS proved its worth during the Third Battle of Kharkov on the Eastern front in spring 1943. The commander of the SS Panzer Corps, the excellent military strategist Paul Hausser, had been instructed by Hitler to "stand fast and fight to the death." Hausser defied Hitler's order and initially withdrew his forces before mounting a counterattack. He broke the Soviet line of defense and advanced on Kharkov. He again disobeyed an order, this time to circle the city, and mounted a direct assault on Kharkov in tandem with Field Marshal von Manstein. After four days of intense street fighting, the Waffen SS recaptured the city.

Amidst the death throes of the Third Reich, as the defeat of Hitler became inevitable, Waffen SS units also served with distinction as emergency reserves held back to counterattack when the Allies broke through the line. Hitler turned to his loyal SS troops to pursue increasingly desperate and impossible operations, such as the "Spring Awakening" mission to recapture Hungarian oil fields in March 1945. Hitler was disgusted when the Waffen SS units failed, claiming that the force "did not fight as the situation demanded." He then issued an order that the Leibstandarte SS Adolf Hitler, his personal bodyguard, should remove its Hitler armbands. The Waffen SS general chose to ignore the order as his men had fought loyally and valiantly in the face of ridiculous odds. While the Waffen SS had fought many battles without great distinction, this specific failure was far from their fault.

Left: A belt buckle featuring the Waffen SS motto, "My Honor is Loyalty," and Nazi insignia

Opposite: In June 1944, the SS murdered 642 unarmed men, women, and children at Oradour-sur-Glane, France, as a reprisal for the kidnapping of a Waffen SS officer by the French Resistance

In the very last throes of the war in Europe, it would be a Waffen SS regiment of Nordic volunteers, the 11th SS Freiwilligen Panzergrenadier Division Nordland, who fought to the end, defending the Reichstag in Berlin in April 1945. It was actions such as these that shaped the Waffen SS's reputation as an elite—and its ranks certainly included some elite warriors. Following the end of the war and the dismantling of the German military forces some of the Waffen SS veterans successfully continued their military career and became a significant element of the French Foreign Legion.

Certain Waffen SS units and individuals sought out danger and adventure, and were reckless in pursuit of their goals; others were evidentially linked to episodes of almost unspeakable cruelty and sadism, including at Oradour-sur-Glane in June 1944. There, SS Sturmbannführer Deikmann ordered the execution of a village's entire male population before torching a church containing all the women and children. Any that tried to flee the flames were gunned down. One woman, Marguerite Rouffanche, escaped through the sacristy window and was shot, but she managed to crawl to the safety of some bushes. She was one of the few survivors: 642 villagers were killed in the slaughter.

It was actions such as this that led to the entire Waffen SS—except post-1943 conscripts—being declared a criminal organization by the International Military Tribunal during the Nuremberg Trials. In terms of the scale of atrocities, the Waffen SS cannot be compared with Allgemeine SS units and particularly the Einsatzkommando, who appeared to undertake their roles of exterminating and terrorizing minorities with unquestioning zeal, but it did play a role in the rounding up of Jews in Eastern Europe. In the chaos of war, the Waffen SS as a whole might not have proved to be a military, ethnic, or ideological elite, but it had played a significant and brutal role in putting fascist ideology into action.

Devil's Brigade

The unique joint American and Canadian commando unit that fought in Italy and France in World War II

Opposite: An M-29 Weasel, the specialist armored snow sleds that were meant to be deployed with the Devil's Brigade on the abortive mission to Norway

"THE BLACK DEVILS are all around us every time we come into the line. We never hear them come." These words were allegedly written in the abandoned diary of a German lieutenant who faced the 1st Special Service Force at Anzio. In the same campaign, a brigade sergeant, Victor Kaisner, heard a German soldier say *Schwarzer Teufel*—"Black Devil"—in the moment before his throat was slit. The name stuck and the 1st Special Service Force became known as the Black Devils or the Devil's Brigade for the rest of its short life in World War II.

No one now knows whether the journal really existed or whether the tale was concocted as part of a clever psychological campaign conducted by the commanding officer of the 1st Special Service Force. Nothing about the Devil's Brigade would turn out to be straightforward. Even the idea for the force was developed by a man who might well be described as a "mad scientist". Then the troops were trained to be an elite ready for airborne, mountainous and snowbound operations in a campaign that evaporated before they

FACT FILE

REGION: Aleutian Islands, Europe

ERA: 1942–44

KEY ENCOUNTERS: Winter Line, Italy 1943; Alezzo 1944; Operation Dragoon 1944

TACTICS AND TECHNIQUES: Commando unit trained for mountain and arctic battle, used for covert assaults and raids

WEAPONRY: M1911A1 pistol; V42 fighting knife; M1A1 carbine; M1 rifle; M2 60mm mortar; portable flamethrower; Browning LMG

LEGACY: One of the principal inspirations for today's special forces in Canada and the United States

Above: Special forces being briefed at Anzio, 1944, where the Devil's Brigade began to earn its reputation for fearless night-time missions and the use of psychological warfare

were ever deployed. Yet they fought with distinction in a different type of war, one for which they had not been specifically trained.

Officially called the 1st Special Service Force, the brigade was a highly unusual joint US and Canadian venture, born out of the enthusiasm of two British men: the aristocratic Admiral Louis Mountbatten, who masterminded the exploits of the British Commandos, and a scientist named Geoffrey Pyke, whose other proposals included making massive aircraft carriers out of the frozen composite material Pykrete, a combination of sawdust and ice. Needless to say, the carriers were never commissioned.

Pyke had come up with a plan to parachute a deep penetration force and snow-tracked vehicles behind enemy lines in order to mount a guerrilla campaign of destruction against Norwegian industry. Norway had fallen under Nazi control, and Germany was benefiting from using the country's resources to aid its own war effort. Pyke figured that knocking out Norway's hydroelectric plants, bridges, tunnels, and rail tracks would help the Allies to cripple Germany. Inspired by polar explorers, the unit's vehicles, called "Weasels," would be fast, mobile, armored snow sleds that could carry weaponry and a small crew. Not only could this new commando force smash Norwegian industry, but if such an incursion were to take place, Pyke argued, German troops would have to be redeployed far behind their own lines to deal with the irritants.

It is something of a surprise that the Americans took Pyke seriously. He wore fancy spats, did not bother with socks, and rarely bathed, shaved, or washed his hair. Without Mountbatten's fulsome support, his idea would have been given short shrift on the other side of the Atlantic, but George C. Marshall, Chief of Staff in Washington DC, reported: "The civilian concerned is a very odd-looking individual, but talks well and may have an important contribution to make."

Just like Merrill's Marauders, the creation of the 1st Special Service Force was authorized in response to a British request to involve its allies in special operations. While the Marauders would be shipped off to India to train to fight the Japanese in the jungles of Burma, Canadian and American soldiers were trained at Fort William Henry Harrison in Helena, Montana, in preparation for Operation Plough, the airborne assault into the cold, dark, and mountainous terrain of Norway. The operation was so secret that many of the recruits had no idea where they were when they arrived in Montana.

They were put under the command of a highly rated young officer, Lieutenant Colonel Robert T. Frederick. However, while the Canadian trainees had been hand-picked for the special operation, many of the initial American recruits were misfits and rejects from other units. Frederick had to put a lot of effort into recruiting superior soldiers for what was likely to be a very difficult mission. In fact, a conversation between Geoffrey Pyke, a representative of the War Department in Washington, DC, and a British brigadier reveals that the US thought that the mission would prove fatal, to the extent that the War Department was not even interested in detailing a plan for the extraction of possible survivors: "I think these are sacrifice troops ... I'd put them down as lost troops and willing to pay for it—if they achieve this." Britain was in agreement. The Brigadier responded, "It's a desperate adventure, all right."

Above: Lieutenant Colonel Robert T. Frederick, who molded the joint brigade of Americans and Canadians into an unorthodox fighting force

Lieutenant Colonel Robert Frederick worked against the odds to create a courageous special forces elite out of his Canadian and American troops. Initial training did not always go well, as the 1st Special Service Force's official war diary entry for 25 August 1942 reveals: "A bad day for jumpers, an unusually large number balked at the door. Casualties were also high compared to previous days. 37 admitted to hosp[ital]."

Just over a month later, by 30 September 1942, the tone of the diary had already undergone a positive change: "This is probably one of the finest groups of men ever assembled, their morale has been extremely high despite the arduous training."

Above: The Devil's Brigade shoulder patch; the unit would leave a note with an image of their insignia and the message "The worst is yet to come" on the bodies of German soldiers they had killed

Opposite: Lord Mountbatten, who oversaw the exploits of the British Commandos in World War II, helped to initiate the 1st Special Service Force in 1942

That training—consisting of learning to drive the Weasels at speed, cross-country marching, skiing, rock-climbing, parachute training, demolitions, shooting practice, hand-to-hand combat, and obstacle courses undertaken with live fire—was conducted over a range of terrains from the prairies of Montana to the waters of Chesapeake Bay and the snowy peaks of the Great Divide. To aid the *esprit de corps*, Canadians and Americans were equally divided into each of the army quarters, and adopted distinctive insignia depicting two crossed arrows and a red badge in the shape of a spearhead.

Then, after all the airborne, mountain, and arctic training for the operation, the Norwegian government in exile vetoed the scheme: the destruction of the Norwegian economy, they rightly asserted, was going to hit their people harder than the Germans. With its operational purpose instantly quashed, the 1st Special Service Force was threatened with immediate dissolution. Frederick, however, was having none of it. By now, he believed that he had created an elite unit that could prove itself in any theatre of war.

Lieutenant Robert M. Stuart, an officer in the brigade who would go on to fight with the Rangers in Korea and work as a covert agent in Europe and Vietnam, agreed, writing later: "We had our screwballs—maybe more than our share ... but they were damn good screwballs, and fighting screwballs. Frederick had the spark to catch our imagination and to turn that screwball oddity into what I think was probably as good a fighting outfit, man for man, as any ever produced in the US Army or any other."

So, the 1st Special Service Force, minus its Weasel vehicles, was finally deployed in World War II in July 1943. First stop were the Aleutian Islands of Alaska in the Pacific, which proved to be something of an anticlimax as not a shot was fired. The real theatre of war soon beckoned, though, when the Force was sent to southern Italy in October. Despite the abandonment of Operation Plough, Mountbatten thought that the 1st Special Service Force would prove to be a great success. On 2 October 1943 he wrote to Geoffrey Pyke: "You must feel proud to think that the force ... has become such a vital necessity in the coming stage of the war."

In Italy, the Force's mountain skills were evident as they scaled an almost vertical escarpment in freezing rain to knock out a German stronghold on Monte La Difensa. The battle was predicted to last up to five days. The Force took the position in two hours. They then continued their treacherous Italian mountain campaign over the winter, incurring losses of around a

thousand dead and wounded, but scoring successes that were beyond the skills of any other unit.

The Force was then transferred to a totally different terrain: the beachhead at Anzio, south of Rome. It was here that would establish themselves as a legendary elite, nicknamed the Devil's Brigade or the Black Devils as they smeared their faces with boot polish for covert night-time operations. Frederick, who was promoted to Brigadier-General in January 1944, enjoyed huge respect within the Force and inspired great loyalty: at Anzio, when one of his patrols was pinned down by machine gun fire in a German minefield, Frederick ran into battle himself to help the stretcher bearers rescue the wounded. Not only brave, he had a gift for psychological warfare. He would continually move trucks around Anzio to give the Germans the impression that they were up against a much larger force. It worked: the Germans thought that the unit of little more than a thousand men was a whole division of more than 10,000 soldiers, not least because of the havoc it was wreaking. After slaying a German, the Devils would leave a card on the corpse bearing an image of the unit's spearhead and the words: "*DAS DICKE ENDE KOMMT NOCH*"—"The worst is yet to come." An order found on a captured German warned that the enemy was "an elite Canadian-American Force. They are treacherous, unmerciful, and clever." The Germans retreated from the area near the beachhead to avoid the Devil's Brigade's killer night patrols that repeatedly raided behind enemy lines.

This operation was followed by service in the Allied offensive towards Rome, where they secured a range of bridges to stop the Germans destroying them as they withdrew, and the Devils were amongst the first Allied units to reach the Italian capital.

In August 1944, the Devil's Brigade entered the final phase of its existence, taking part in invasion of southern France in Operation Dragoon and becoming co-opted into the 1st Airborne Task Force. They fought in southern France until December 1944, when the now depleted Force, having never taken part in the operation it was created to undertake and having outlived its role as a commando unit, was disbanded. Many of the remaining soldiers were reassigned to airborne and Ranger units. Some US troops, though, joined the 474th Infantry Regiment which undertook occupation duties in Norway. A handful of the Devil's Brigade finally made it to their original destination.

As an official unit-level cooperation between two different countries, the Devil's Brigade is almost unique in the history of modern warfare. The force of 1,800 men accounted for 12,000 German casualties and took 7,000 prisoners in the space of just 16 months' active service, and received a Distinguished Unit Citation. In 2013, the United States Congress passed a special bill so that it could award this dual nationality force the Congressional Gold Medal. As an innovative North American special force, they inspired the Green Berets as well as the Canadian Special Operations Regiment.

Above: An Allied soldier climbing over rubble in a wrecked street, in Anzio, 1944, which was the scene of heavy fighting and covert Devil's Brigade operations

Merrill's Marauders

The courageous US military unit in WWII who battled against Japanese troops and hostile conditions in the Burmese jungle

CAPTAIN FRED O. LYONS, on his return from the jungles of Burma, wanted to tell the truth about the exploits of his fellow band of elite soldiers. "I was one of Merrill's Marauders," he told interviewer Paul Wilder in 1945. "I was one of those who marched that thousand miles through hell to slash the hamstrings of the Japanese armies in Burma."

On 24 February 1944, 2,750 American soldiers began a long march from India, over the Himalayas, and into the jungles of Burma to fight behind Japanese lines in World War II. Once there, they were continually outnumbered, fought over 30 engagements including five major battles in just a few months, and suffered from disease and malnutrition in horrendous conditions, but they refused to stop. As well as dysentery, "Other illnesses broke out among the men—yellow jaundice, malaria, stomach disorders," said Captain Lyons, "but we kept plugging on. Our goal was Myitkyina, and we hated to quit before we got there." After the successful completion of their almost insane mission, every single one of Merrill's Marauders would be awarded a Bronze Star. And yet

FACT FILE

REGION: Southeast Asia

ERA: 1943–44

KEY ENCOUNTERS: Walawbum 1944; Nhpum Ga 1944; Myitkyina 1944

TACTICS AND TECHNIQUES: Lightly equipped long-range penetration unit used in jungle warfare

WEAPONRY: Thompson submachine gun; M1903A4 sniper rifle; bazooka; mortar; machete/kukri knife

LEGACY: Vital to Allied progress in Southeast Asia in World War II

Above: Merrill's Marauders with Chinese troops on the Ledo Road, an Allied supply route through Burma, 1944

some back home in the US had accused them of cracking up and refusing to fight on; this was why Lyons felt the need to put the record straight.

At the Quebec Conference of August 1943, President Franklin D. Roosevelt and Prime Minister Winston Churchill agreed a plan to create an American unit to lead the Chinese Army in the war against the Japanese in Burma. This would be a long-range penetration mission behind enemy lines with the aim of disrupting the enemy's supply lines and communications, and reopening the Allies' own supply lines along the Burma Road. Without this activity it seemed unlikely that the Allies would win the war in the East.

Roosevelt called for existing US Army soldiers to volunteer for a "dangerous and hazardous mission." The troop was designated the 5307th Composite Unit (Provisional) and given the codename "Galahad," although a *Times* of London journalist dubbed them "Merrill's Marauders" after their Brigadier General, Frank Merrill, and the name stuck. Almost 3,000 soldiers signed up, some of whom had experienced jungle warfare in Central America

Above: Merrill's Marauders on a jungle trail in Burma, where they repeatedly defeated the Japanese despite suffering from increasingly harsh conditions, disease, malnutrition, and dysentery

and the Pacific. However, one veteran described the unit as "having more than their fair share of drunkards, derelicts, guardhouse graduates, men of low intelligence, and out-and-out bad men." Yet, somehow this rough and ready force was to serve with valor and distinction over the course of five months in hell.

The men were sent to India to take part in a tough training regime, learning from the British Army's own long-range jungle unit, the Chindits, but also drawing on American history: "Day and night we marched, ran, hid, feinted, learned all over again the lessons that first had been learned by American frontiersmen in their struggle with the Indians," recalled Lyons. "We became hard as our green helmets, tough as our green GI brogans. I weighed 146 pounds and there wasn't an ounce of fat on me." As well as undergoing tough endurance training, they learned jungle-fighting skills and long-range penetration tactics.

The men were allocated jungle boots and a curved kukri blade to clear paths, along with machine-guns, pistols, and mortars. They were then sent off to march 1,000 miles on foot into the most inhospitable theater of war possible, without any heavy-weapons support and without proper rations. Their general was the formidable "Vinegar" Joe Stilwell, who decided that the soldiers could survive on normal ration packs even though they would be marching day after day in the searing temperatures and suffocating

Below: A C-47 cargo transport crash lands after finally managing to drop supplies to the isolated 101st Airborne Division, which repulsed German attempts to capture Bastogne, 1944. Like Merrill's Marauders, the 101st was also awarded the Distinguished Unit Citation

DISTINGUISHED UNIT CITATIONS

MERRILL'S MARAUDERS, WHICH existed as a unit for less than a year, joined the likes of the 101st Airborne Division in being awarded the Distinguished Unit Citation for the whole unit's extraordinary heroism in the field. To be given the award: "The unit must display such gallantry, determination, and *esprit de corps* in accomplishing its mission under extremely difficult and hazardous conditions as to set it apart and above other units participating in the same campaign."

Above: (Top) General Joseph "Vinegar Joe" Stilwell and General Frank Merrill in Burma, 1944 (Below) Stilwell with Curtis LeMay, who directed air operations against the Japanese in China

humidity of the jungle. They were accompanied by 700 pack animals, some of which were mules, but hundreds of them were Australian Waler horses that were completely unsuited to the jungle climate. Not one horse survived the mission.

Solidiers died on the route. Some plummeted down cliff faces on narrow mountain passes, and the Marauders had to repeatedly cross and re-cross rivers and wade through silt banks lined with impenetrable terrain. Most made it behind enemy lines and began to mount operations against the Japanese, including roadblocks that disrupted supply lines. An early success was the battle for the Kamaing Road at Walawbum, which they had secured by the beginning of March 1944.

Usually outnumbered, the Marauders proved to be an adept fighting elite that utilized their superb marksmanship to surprise the attacking Japanese forces. Lyons described one of the numerous encounters: "Jap bodies were piled so deep after the fourth wave had been cut down that, during a lull in the fighting, Cadamo had to sneak out and kick some of them out of the way to clear the range for his gun. In front of another gun I counted bodies seven deep. At last came a wait that stretched into hours with no more Japs coming up that bloody hill. The strain began to tell as the men flopped into their holes. The fight was over."

The battalion pressed on into Burma, trudging along ridges and down into the jungle. At the end of March, General Stilwell called on the Marauders to take a defensive position and block the area of Nhpum Ga, a strategy the penetration unit was neither trained nor equipped to undertake. A third of the Marauders were cut off by the Japanese forces in the major battle that followed.

Lacking clean water and fighting to survive on meager rations, the troops were trapped for days and peppered with wave after wave of mortar fire that killed both men and pack animals. Captain Lyons was one of those trapped: "They began to call the ridge Maggot Hill as the carcasses of horses inside the perimeter decayed and the stench of dead Japs outside it became more and more violent." The Marauders held firm but were stuck for 15 days until the Chinese army broke the Japanese stranglehold. By then only 89 of the trapped troop's 400 pack animals were still alive. The Marauders had killed over 500 Japanese and lost only 57 themselves, but 300 were wounded and another 300 were knocked out by illness or exhaustion.

After two months of intense action in the field, the Marauders should have been withdrawn, but Vinegar Joe insisted that they should march onwards to their ultimate goal: the airfield at Myitkyina. The action, conditions, and lack of supplies had taken their toll. By this point, Lyons recalled, "I had amoebic dysentery. The medics were of the opinion I had contracted it when I drank water out of the elephant tracks ... I had lost a considerable quantity of blood to leeches, those horrifying grayish-brown parasites that bury their heads in your veins and suck till they are bloated several times larger than normal size with your blood."

The rainy season had begun, making conditions even more difficult, but still the exhausted, malnourished, and sick troops pushed forward, endlessly plunging back and forth across rivers, hacking their way through the dense jungle and climbing over another mountain range. Even Frank Merrill, who had shared the hardships of the campaign with his troops, fell by the wayside, suffering a heart attack and catching malaria. To the

Above: The badge of Merrill's Marauders, whose official title was 5307th Composite Unit (Provisional)

Above: General Joseph Stilwell and Colonel Charles Hunter of Merrill's Marauders talking to a patrol leader who has conducted reconnaissance near the Japanese stronghold at Myitkyina, 17 May 1944

list of diseases ravaging the force was added scrub typhus. The remaining 1,300 Marauders were constantly assaulted by reinforced Japanese troops and snipers. Lyons reported: "By now my dysentery was so violent I was draining blood. Every one of the men was sick from one cause or another." He could no longer even carry his pack while on patrol, but somehow the men continued to score victories against the odds in repeated skirmishes with the enemy: "Then the gun spoke. Down flopped a half-dozen Japs, then another half dozen. The column spewed from their marching formation into the bush. We grabbed up the gun and slid back into the jungle. Sometimes staggering, sometimes running, sometimes dragging, I made it back to camp ... All I wanted was unconsciousness."

The Marauders were in their final hour: "As we finished each job it looked as though we'd be relieved; then we'd have one more job to do." In preparation for the battle to take the Japanese stronghold of Myitkyina, Stilwell sent the Marauders on a grueling 65-mile march through the jungle at the height of monsoon season to perform a flanking maneuver. The battle "was the straw that broke the Marauders' back," Lyon said. They took the airfield, but, "We just couldn't take it anymore. Faster and faster our men began dropping—from wastage of disease, yes, but mostly from exhaustion." The dysentery had become so bad that some soldiers cut out the seat of their pants so that they could continue firing while relieving themselves.

Once again Stilwell was using a lightly equipped unconventional force—exhausted from their long penetration mission—to carry out conventional warfare. He also refused to follow standard medical evacuation procedure and forced 200 Marauders to leave their sickbeds and report for duty. In the Battle of Myitkyina alone 272 Marauders died, with many more injured.

As the battle to take the town from 4,500 Japanese soldiers continued, Chinese reinforcements arrived and many Marauders, including Lyons, were finally taken out of the line and hospitalized for treatment. "Not a man of the Marauders went back to India a walking, well man," claimed Lyons. He was not exaggerating. Of the 2,750 men who had entered Burma, only two surviving soldiers had not been hospitalized with disease or wounds. Myitkyina was finally secured in early August 1944, with only 200 Marauders still standing. Mission accomplished, Merrill's Marauders, the 5307th Composite Unit (Provisional), was disbanded on 10 August 1944.

Even as the Marauders lay on their sickbeds, Stilwell wanted them to volunteer to return to the jungle. None did, which led to claims that they had somehow cracked. Lyons countered: "Merrill's Marauders—all of us who can still walk—would march another such thousand miles to meet the Jap, if that were our mission. No, the morale of Merrill's Marauders never ended. We never backed down. We just wore out!"

The US Army knew just what the Marauders had achieved against all odds. The unit had been sent on a suicide mission: the military authorities secretly thought virtually no one would return. As well as every soldier being awarded the Bronze Star, the force was given a Distinguished Unit Citation.

THE GERMAN TANK MASTERS

Panzer Lehr

The German armored division feared as the most elite tank force in World War II, which hampered the Allied advance following the D-Day landings

THE PANZER LEHR was a German armored division famous for the quality of its soldiers and its armored vehicles, and for providing stubborn resistance against overwhelming numbers following the D-Day landings in Normandy. In the end, though, it was crippled by a combination of the obduracy of the American infantry—in particular the 101st Airborne Division—and Allied airpower during the Normandy campaign and the Battle of the Bulge. The legend of the 101st's Easy Company, the famed Band of Brothers, was made all the greater because the Germans that they held out against for so long included the Panzer Lehr division.

The Panzer Lehr was held in such esteem because it comprised highly decorated veterans that had gone on to teach armored skills at the military academies Panzertruppenschule 1 and Panzertruppenschule 2 ("*Panzer*" means armor and "*Lehr*" teach): they were regarded as the crème de la crème. With Germany preparing for the Allied invasion of Normandy, Hitler needed an elite mobile armored force comprising his very best tank commanders, so the instructors were brought on to the frontline. They were given Germany's best tanks and armored

FACT FILE

REGION: Europe

ERA: 1944–45

KEY ENCOUNTERS: Caen 1944; Saint-Lô 1944; Battle of the Bulge 1944–5

TACTICS AND TECHNIQUES: Tank unit favoring devastating, rapid assaults

WEAPONRY: Panther; Panzer IV; Tiger I and II

LEGACY: Elite armored division made vulnerable by Germany's weakened air force

vehicles, including the famed Panzer IV and the even more impressive Panther. Throughout World War II, the Allies could not fully match the tank-power of the Germans, who had managed to combine armored strength, firepower, and mobility within a single vehicle. The Fireflys, the upgraded British Sherman tanks, were effective, but it was only the United States' Shermans, mounted with a 76 mm M1 tank gun, that were equal to the German tanks, and they were not introduced until the last throes of the war in Europe.

The Panzer Lehr, which is sometimes referred to as the 130-Panzer-Lehr-Division because many of its units which were assigned the number 130, was put together over the winter of 1943-44 and sent to France in readiness for the anticipated Allied invasion. Together with new *Schützenpanzerwagens* (half-track armored cars) for reconnaissance, 237 of the latest model Panther, Panzer IV and Tiger tanks were assigned to the division. The Panzer Lehr also included the 316th Radio-Controlled Panzer Company, which was responsible for operating one of Germany's secret innovations: unmanned remote-controlled armored vehicles that were to be loaded with explosives and driven up to enemy fortifications, where they would be detonated.

Above: A German Panther is repaired in Russia during World War II

The importance of the division was underlined by the appointment of Lieutenant General Fritz Bayerlein, who had been Field Marshal Erwin Rommel's Chief of Staff in North Africa, as its commander.

Following the Allied invasion of Normandy on 6 June 1944, the Panzer Lehr began its first operation against the British and Canadian forces on 8 June around Caen. It immediately proved successful, slowing down British progress, and even managed to counter a flanking maneuver at the Battle of Villers-Bocage, leading to a temporary British withdrawal.

The Panzer Lehr may have slowed up the British at Caen, but it was eventually forced to withdraw in the face of huge opposition. It continued to help stymie the Allied advance in northern France throughout June while

Above: Panzers being transported en masse to the Eastern front, 1943

suffering huge losses, including 3,000 casualties and around 50 tanks, in the barrage of Allied aerial attacks. Germany's inability to match Allied aerial strength in the later stages of the war would prove decisive. No matter how good elite divisions such as Panzer Lehr proved to be on the ground, when the skies were clear they were vulnerable from above.

At the beginning of July 1944, the division was sent to meet the American advance around Saint-Lô. Although the terrain of small hedged fields and groves of trees inhibited its maneuverability, the division managed to capture Pont-Hébert and hold off American counterattacks. Once again, the Panzer Lehr proved itself to be one of the best armored divisions ever known in the history of warfare, but it could not protect itself from aerial assault, and the Allies' M10 tank destroyers were also making inroads. The Panzer Lehr was forced to withdraw, having lost another 20 tanks, but worse was to come. The division lay directly in the path of the huge assault named Operation Cobra.

It had fought valiantly since its introduction to the theatre of war, and the *Wehrmachtbericht*, the daily armed forces report on Nazi radio, reported in July 1944: "In the fight against three of the best British divisions, the Panzer Lehr Division, led by Lieutenant General Bayerlein, has proven to be excellent." However, it could no longer stand in the way of massive artillery bombardment and the advance of nearly 150,000 enemy troops. The division limped from the frontline with just 20 remaining tanks. Many of Germany's best tank commanders had died.

The division was refitted and remanned back in Germany. By the middle of December it was ready for the major German operation, *Die Wacht am Rhein* (The Watch on the Rhine), known to the Allies as the Battle of the Bulge, conducted in the Ardennes forests of Belgium, Luxembourg, and France. It was Hitler's last throw of the dice in the desperate attempt to stop Allied progress towards Germany, and the Panzer Lehr was chosen to hold the center of the line.

One of the initial aims of the operation was to take Bastogne, where many of the major roads of the Ardennes converged: without access to Bastogne, Allied progress would be severely hampered and the Germans could push forward to take Antwerp. The Panzer Lehr was given the task of taking Bastogne. The 28th Infantry Division of the US Army had fought hard in the area but was completely decimated by the influx of the huge German force, leaving Bastogne vulnerable. The 101st Airborne Division, known as the Screaming Eagles, which was recovering from two months of fighting in the Netherlands, was pushed forward to fill the gap. General Dwight Eisenhower

Above: The US Army 101st Airborne Division watch a resupply of Bastogne, where the "Screaming Eagles" held out against German units supported by the Panzer Lehr, 1944

Above: Refugees being evacuated from Bastogne, the pivotal crossroads that the Panzer Lehr failed to secure

called Bastogne "the place that has to be held no matter what." As the 101st Airborne approached the town, beleaguered American troops were flooding in the other direction, but the division moved forward with bravura. Captain G. William Sefton of the 501st Parachute Infantry Regiment said: "I remember this short, stubby sergeant from the 28th Division, which of course had taken the brunt of the attack … standing there with no weapon, saying, 'Go back, go back, there's a million of them out there.' Our guys: 'Oh hell, don't worry about it. We're 101st Airborne. We'll take care of it.' And remarkably, they did, but not before enduring hell out in the woods of Bastogne."

The 101st Airborne got to Bastogne before the Panzer Lehr Division and dug in to protect the all-important crossroads, but they were soon encircled. Sefton recalled: "That's when a paratrooper made the immortal remark: 'Well, they've got us surrounded, the poor bastards.'" Fritz Bayerlein, the Panzer Lehr commander, was about to meet his match.

The US division faced continual bombardment and assaults from the Panzer Lehr and the 26th Volksgrenadier, but still they held out. German General Heinrich Freiherr von Lüttwitz had seen enough. He sent a letter to General Anthony McCauliffe, who was acting commander of the 101st Airborne: "There is only one possibility to save the encircled USA troops from total annihilation: that is the honorable surrender of the encircled town." McCauliffe sent the German commander just one word by way of reply: "NUTS."

The Panzer Lehr assaulted nearby Dinant, but clear skies left it vulnerable to air attack and it took heavy casualties, falling back to Bastogne. Meanwhile the German artillery continued the bombardment of the 101st Airborne. Bill Guarnere, who lost a leg while attempting to save a colleague, remembered:

THE SECRET WEAPON

ONE OF THE Panzer divisions' most effective secret weapons in World War II was not a piece of machinery, but a tank commander, SS-Obersturmführer Michael Wittmann. He fought with the Heavy SS-Panzer Battalion 101, which supported the Panzer Lehr position at the Battle of Villers-Bocage on 13 June 1944. His crew almost single-handedly fought off a British flanking maneuver. As the British attacked, he recalled, "I had no time to assemble my company; instead I had to act quickly, as I had to assume that the enemy had already spotted me and would destroy me where I stood. I set off with one tank and passed the order to the others not to retreat a single step but to hold their ground." During a 15-minute episode in the midst of the battle, he knocked out 14 tanks, 15 personnel carriers and two anti-tank guns with his Tiger tank. Wittmann was personally credited with the destruction of 138 tanks and 132 anti-tank guns during the course of the war. He became a household name in Germany and was awarded the Knight's Cross of the Iron Cross with Oak Leaves and Swords, but the Allies were unaware that this single tank commander was responsible for so much carnage. He was killed on 8 August 1944 when his tank was destroyed by a Sherman Firefly.

"The most intense I ever went through—shelling—the most intense in the world ... unmerciful shelling ... everything was just shredded." The isolated 101st Airborne could not be relieved and the soldiers tried to protect themselves in foxholes dug in the snow and frozen ground.

J.B. Stokes of Easy Company, 506th Parachute Infantry, recalled for the *Band of Brothers* television series: "It was the most miserable place I've been in my life. Even today on a real cold night, we go to bed and my wife'll tell you the first thing I'll say is that I'm glad I'm not in Bastogne." They were running out of both food and ammunition as air drops either could not get through or missed them, falling into the hands of the Germans.

Below: The monument to "Easy Company," 506th Parachute Infantry Regiment, who defied the odds at Bastogne

Towards the end, Machine Gunner J.B. Price was beginning to despair: "I had half a belt of ammunition left and two shells of a carbine and I done made up my mind that one of those shells in the carbine was for me." But

that morning the skies were clear enough for Allied aircraft to mount a major bombardment of the German positions and C47 Dakotas dropped supplies to the men of the 101st Airborne. General Patton's Third Army was finally able to mount a ground assault to relieve the division. They drove a corridor straight through the Panzer Lehr position to reach Bastogne. The beleaguered Panzer Lehr counterattacked to close the corridor but failed and was withdrawn. Meanwhile, a sign had gone up in town: "Bastogne: Bastion of the Battered Bastards of the 101st."

The Panzer Lehr was refitted one last time, but it was no longer the elite, well-trained, and well-equipped force of summer 1944. Nonetheless it fought well against the US 9th Armored Division at Remagen in Germany, in March 1945, before the remnant of the division surrendered a month later, having been encircled by the Allies in the Ruhr Pocket.

Special Air Service

The British SAS, which brought special forces to new heights of respect during the televised Iranian Embassy crisis in London, 1980

"GENTLEMEN, THE BOY STIRLING is mad. Quite, quite mad. But in war there is a place for mad people." So said Field Marshal Montgomery about David Stirling, the founder of the British Special Air Service, who had suggested taking his fledgling unit on a seemingly impossible mission far behind enemy lines in Libya to attack the Tripoli-Tobruk road during World War II.

The Special Air Service began life as nothing more than a work of fiction invented to trick the Germans into thinking that a force of enemy paratroopers was working in the Middle East and North Africa. David Stirling made that myth a reality in 1941 when he created the L Detachment of the imaginary regiment to conduct covert operations in the North African desert. And in time that reality would become almost mythical once more, as the SAS attained legendary status throughout the world.

The SAS's early operations were the result of the 8th Army's initial inability to stop Erwin Rommel and his German and Italian forces from sweeping across North Africa. Their first mission was a disaster. One night in November 1941, 62 soldiers were parachuted behind enemy lines, with the intention that they would then make

FACT FILE

REGION: Worldwide

ERA: 1941–present day

KEY ENCOUNTERS: Malayan Emergency 1952; Aden 1964-7; Dhofar 1970-77; Iranian Embassy 1980; Falklands 1982; Afghanistan 2001

TACTICS AND TECHNIQUES: Covert unit for deep penetration behind enemy lines; anti-terrorist activities

WEAPONRY: 8 carbine; M16, HK G3 and G36 rifles; sniper rifles; HK MP5 submachine gun

LEGACY: One of the best special forces units in the world

their way on foot to destroy airfields at Gazala and Timimi in Libya. However, the parachutists were dropped straight into one of the strongest gales ever known in the area and the operation dissolved into chaos, with 40 of the soldiers killed or captured.

Undeterred, Stirling set up a unit of around 100 men to work behind enemy lines and conducted an incisive, clever, and vicious campaign against German airfields, fuel dumps, infrastructure, and communications. Rather than relying on parachutes, he acquired some US Army jeeps in July 1942 and stripped them down to their bare essentials, allowing for speed and mobility while still carrying enough resources for long-range operations within enemy territory.

Mike Sadler was on one of those early excursions: a jeep raid on an important German airfield at Fuka in Egypt in 1942. As he told Sean Rayment for the book *Tales from the Special Forces Club*, the 18 jeeps drove straight into the airfield in a surprise attack: "the attack went in with all guns blazing. The weight of fire was incredible and must have been quite deadly." They wasted no time shooting up the airfield, planes, and German soldiers. "It wasn't a battle as such, just a quick raid which really didn't last more than about 10 minutes. Only one of our chaps was hit and killed on the field ... and we destroyed 20 or 30 aircraft."

Stirling was developing a new breed of unconventional, brave, and elite soldier who would go beyond normal means to cripple the enemy. Sadler

Below: C Squadron of the SAS in Rhodesia (now Zimbabwe) in 1954; the SAS is deployed on special overseas missions and training exercises throughout the world

Above: The Special Air Service in North Africa. Created in 1943, the SAS helped initiate the modern era of unconventional soldiery

Opposite: The Special Air Service during its first campaign in North Africa during World War II

recalled being with a new recruit, Lieutenant David Russell, on a desert reconnaissance mission behind enemy lines when their jeep took a puncture and they had no pump to fix it. Russell, a fluent German speaker, asked Sadler to drive him to a German anti-tank battery, where he claimed he was an undercover officer and needed a pump urgently. Not only did the German commander give him a pump, but he showed him around the battery: "but every time the officer's back was turned David took a Lewes bomb from his pack and placed it on one of the guns." After the two SAS men had left, they found the pump did not fit, but they had the satisfaction of hearing the bombs exploding in the distance.

The SAS was soon given full regiment status and continued to harass the Germans behind enemy lines, destroying 250 aircraft as well as many ammunition and fuel dumps during the Allied campaign in North Africa. The principles had been set for the SAS's postwar activity, where its tough, daring, and resilient soldiers would work covertly to collect intelligence, commit acts of sabotage, and carry out raids behind enemy lines.

Like many elite units it was disbanded at the end of World War II in 1945, but the necessity for a permanent special force soon became obvious and it was re-formed permanently in 1947. The *esprit de corps* of the regiment was enhanced by its adoption of a sand-colored beret, its insignia of the flaming sword Excalibur (often referred to as a winged dagger) and the motto "Who Dares Wins." The team spirit was soon put to good effect in secret operations in the Malayan Emergency of 1952, followed by deployment to Borneo and Aden during extended troubles in the 1960s.

By spring 1970, when a batch of would-be recruits including Peter Winner (the pseudonym of an SAS veteran who wishes to remain anonymous) attended Bradbury Lines, the SAS's base in Hereford, the regiment had become particularly famous for the harsh rigors of its selection policy and training. The SAS, just like in its early days, draws men from the very best of the regular army. As

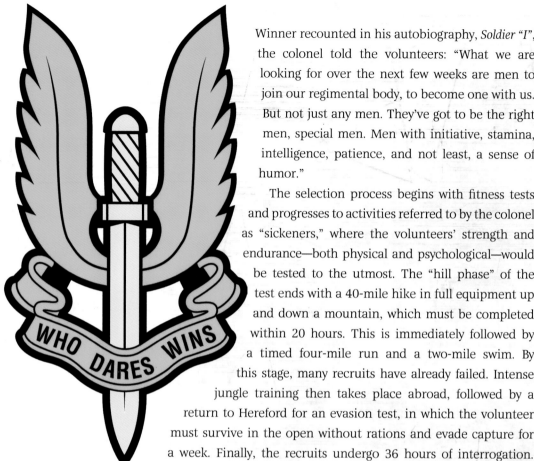

Above: The "Who Dares Wins" motto of the SAS, lauded as the model for other special forces units including Delta Force

Opposite: An SAS gunman creeps stealthily along the balcony of the Iranian Embassy, London, during the hostage siege of 1980

Winner recounted in his autobiography, *Soldier "I"*, the colonel told the volunteers: "What we are looking for over the next few weeks are men to join our regimental body, to become one with us. But not just any men. They've got to be the right men, special men. Men with initiative, stamina, intelligence, patience, and not least, a sense of humor."

The selection process begins with fitness tests and progresses to activities referred to by the colonel as "sickeners," where the volunteers' strength and endurance—both physical and psychological—would be tested to the utmost. The "hill phase" of the test ends with a 40-mile hike in full equipment up and down a mountain, which must be completed within 20 hours. This is immediately followed by a timed four-mile run and a two-mile swim. By this stage, many recruits have already failed. Intense jungle training then takes place abroad, followed by a return to Hereford for an evasion test, in which the volunteer must survive in the open without rations and evade capture for a week. Finally, the recruits undergo 36 hours of interrogation. Only approximately 15 per cent of volunteers, all of whom regard themselves as top soldiers at the outset, make it through the selection process. Peter Winner passed the selection and went on to complete the tough continuation, parachute, and combat survival training, which in the end would lead him to the Iranian Embassy in 1980 and the Falklands in 1982.

Winner's abilities were put to the test just two years after graduating, in Operation Storm on 19 July 1972. His unit of eight SAS soldiers had to fight off 300 communist insurgents at Mirbat in Dhofar, Oman, to prevent the area's oil lines from falling into enemy hands. The SAS soldiers were covertly operating as a "British Army Training Team (BATT)," aiding the Omani government in its battle against the guerillas of the Popular Front for the Liberation of the Occupied Arabian Gulf. As the guerillas approached the building, they bombarded it with mortars and AK47 gunfire. An SAS staff sergeant, Talaiasi Lababala from Fiji, made a daring breakout to run about 900 yards under

Above: The tough SAS selection system and unorthodox training techniques have been copied by special forces worldwide

fire and single-handedly man a 25-pound gun, which would usually require an entire team to operate, to help repel the assault. He managed to pound the approaching enemy, but would later be shot and killed, and Trooper Tommy Tobin, who went to his aid, would also later die from his wounds. The remaining seven SAS soldiers, including Winner, held off the attack until air support and reinforcements arrived.

It remains one of the operations for which the regiment is most proud, but virtually no one else has heard about it: there has never been an official history of the SAS's top-secret activities in Dhofar. The SAS even lied about the details of the death of Tommy Tobin at a coroner's court in the UK, as the British government couldn't admit that its troops had been involved in a direct confrontation overseas. This was the way of the SAS, as the colonel said at Peter Winner's induction: "No publicity, no media. We move in silently, do our job and melt away into the background."

The highly secretive regiment continued to carry out its covert duties across the world in the 1970s, particularly in Northern Ireland, until, in 5 May 1980, it was caught right in the media spotlight. The siege of the Iranian Embassy in London was conducted in front of the world's news crews. It would prove to be one of the most celebrated special forces operations ever undertaken anywhere in the world.

On 30 April, a terrorist group, fighting for sovereignty for the south Iranian area of Kuzestan and demanding the release of Arab prisoners, had taken over the Iranian Embassy and were holding 26 hostages. On the sixth day of the siege, the hostage-takers grew frustrated with the lack of progress in negotiations and killed one of the hostages, spurring the British into using unconventional means to end the crisis and secure the freedom of the remaining hostages. As a result, the SAS was mobilized into action under codename Operation Nimrod.

Part of standard SAS training takes place in the "Killing House" in Hereford, where soldiers are trained to enter a building under live fire, assess the danger in each room in milliseconds and take out the enemy. Those skills were transferred to live action at the embassy. While the early events of the siege unfolded, the troops had been studying the embassy building plans and undertaking rehearsals in a London barracks.

When the order came for action, one team of four SAS soldiers abseiled from the embassy roof and smashed through the windows, while another team dropped a stun grenade from a skylight. At the same moment, another team of abseilers detonated second-storey windows and more stormed through the back door. The raid was captured on live television, including footage of one hostage, Sim Harris, escaping from a blown-out window and walking along a parapet to safety. In the 17-minute operation, the SAS killed

SPECIAL BOAT SERVICE

LESS FAMOUS THAN the Special Air Service, the UK's Special Boat Service is nonetheless among the best of the world's special forces elites. It slightly predates the SAS, having originally formed as the Special Boat Section in 1940 during World War II. The SBS is effectively the British Navy's version of the SAS, drawing its members mostly from the Royal Marines, and focusing more exclusively on amphibious operations. In 1990 the SBS conducted its own equivalent of the Iranian Embassy operation when a team abseiled from helicopters to liberate the British Embassy in Kuwait during the Gulf War. Surprisingly the SBS played a significant role in the 2001 invasion of Afghanistan—a landlocked country—including at the Battle of Tora Bora. In 2012, the SBS mounted a covert operation in Nigeria to free a Briton and an Italian held hostage by the Islamist extremists Boko Haram. All the terrorists were killed, but both hostages were found dead.

five of the six terrorists and later discovered the other one pretending to be a hostage. All the remaining hostages, except a second civilian killed by the terrorists, were rescued, and the SAS incurred no fatalities.

The action enhanced the SAS's reputation, and its "Who Dares Wins" motto became famous throughout the world. Books and films followed, but this was not the type of exposure the covert unit wanted. Its soldiers now have to agree to special disclosure terms to prevent them revealing the operational secrets of the regiment after they retire. However, in an age of increasing terrorist activities, special forces in other countries saw in the televised embassy raid, just what they required and have since upped their game to try and match the abilities of this elite unit.

Governments around the world have called on the SAS in moments of crises. In the Gambia in 1981, the regiment played a part in restoring the elected government following an attempted coup. In the Falklands War a year later, the SAS mounted a raid on Argentinian aircraft based at Pebble Beach, and also provided invaluable intelligence from behind enemy lines to aid air strikes and battle maneuvers.

The regiment has played a more recent role in the conflicts in the Middle East. It went behind enemy lines to hunt down and neutralize missile units in western Iraq in the Gulf War of 1990, and operated in the wars in both Iraq and Afghanistan, even successfully raiding Taliban headquarters in the latter.

Today, each small team within the SAS has demolition and signals experts, and they are trained to be masters at mountain warfare, amphibious assault, covert operations, anti-terrorist activities, and hostage situations. To aid covert entry into hotspots, they are highly trained in abseiling and the use of High Altitude, Low Opening (HALO) parachutes, freefalling to just 2,000 feet before opening the chute.

The troops are aided in their activities by the very best technology, weapons and armor, but, as SAS veteran Andy McNab says: "If you think of the guys running around in body armor and helmets in Afghanistan today, spare a thought too for [Peter Winner] and his fellow soldiers [in Dhofar, 1972]. Apart from their weapons, the only kit back then was a pair of shorts and desert boots. Remarkably, they still managed to win through." However modern warfare and technology change, it remains the quality of the men in the SAS that makes the regiment so feared and respected throughout the world.

Left: Statue of Sir David Stirling in Doune, Scotland; the founder of the SAS created the unit for covert desert missions behind enemy lines in World War II

Brigade of Gurkhas

The fearsome Nepalese troops who have fought for the British for 200 years, and whose favored weapon is the kukri knife

"I SHOUTED LOUDLY at them to stop, but once they heard my voice one of them started to shoot at me." It was 4 a.m., 22 March 2013, and Rifleman Tuljung Gurung was reaching the end of his guard duty when he saw two men running his direction. He was in a sangar – a 12-foot high wire and fabric guard tower – watching over the gates of the British Patrol Base Sparta in Nahr-e Saraj, Helmand Province, Afghanistan.

The two armed individuals were running at him from a disused compound less than a hundred yards away. As bullets from an AK47 hit the sangar, Gurung returned fire, but one of the enemy rounds hit his helmet, knocking him to the floor. He got to his feet, but the bullet that struck him was just the aperitif: a grenade landed in the guard tower right beside him. Despite his concussion, he acted on instinct and managed to get the grenade out of the sangar just before it detonated. The explosion knocked him down once more and sprayed the sangar with shrapnel and dirt. One of the insurgents was now climbing up the guard tower, ready to finish him off. "I saw him face-to-face,"

FACT FILE

REGION: Indian subcontinent and East Asia
ERA: 1947–present day
KEY ENCOUNTERS: Malayan Emergency 1950s; Indonesia Confrontation 1963–66; Falklands War 1982; Afghanistan 2007–12
TACTICS AND TECHNIQUES: Light infantry
WEAPONRY: Kukri knife; standard issue British Army SA80 rifle; Glock 17 pistol
LEGACY: An enduring remnant of the British Empire that continues to have an elite military role

recalled Gurung. "He was quite a lot bigger than me ... He was so close I didn't get a chance to swing my rifle and injure him, but I suddenly realized I had my kukri knife in my [body armor] so I took it out and started to hit him with it." He was spurred on by instinctive self-preservation and a desire to do his duty: "If I am alive I can save my colleagues. I have to do something. So, like a madman, I did everything."

As Gurung and the attacker fought hand-to-hand, they fell from the 12-foot guard tower and hit the ground. The battered and bruised soldier continued to strike with his knife until both the insurgents fled the scene. Having single-handedly prevented an armed attack on the soldiers sleeping in the patrol base, while showing complete disregard for his own safety, the courageous rifleman was awarded the Military Cross in the operational honours list announced in October 2013.

Above: A Gurkha fighting in the jungles of Burma during World War II

Tuljung Gurung, now a Lance Corporal, is a Gurkha serving in the British Army. His tale is just one of thousands of examples of the heroism of the Gurkhas, who are respected and feared throughout the world for their courage, toughness, loyalty, and resolve to win. The Gurkha motto is "Better to die than be a coward," and they can be heard shouting *"Jai Mahakali, ayo Gorkhali!"* ("Victory to the goddess of war, the Ghurkhas are here!") as they go into battle. The Brigade's insignia includes two crossed kukri knifes, the strong curved blades that have become synonymous with the Gurkhas and are still used in close quarter battle to this day.

The Gurkhas of Nepal are an old-fashioned elite like the Varangian Guard in the Byzantine Empire or Napoleon's Polish Lancers: they are an ethnically selected foreign force fighting for another country. However, those elites were mercenaries and the Gurkhas are a full part of the British Army. The association started 200 years ago in 1814 when the British colonial force in India, the army of the East India Company, found themselves retreating in the face of expert kukri-wielding fighters in the north. The British won the ensuing war, but were so impressed by the courage and skill of the Gurkhas that they started recruiting them into their own army. They became an elite troop used particularly effectively in the mountainous terrain along the Northwest frontier with Afghanistan.

The Gurkhas became a formal, regimented part of the British Indian Army and remained loyal to the British cause in the Indian Mutiny of 1857-58. The mutiny was an insurrection led by Indian soldiers in the British colonial army. The Gurkhas' 2nd Sirmoor Rifles mounted the gallant defense of Hindu Rao's residence in Delhi, losing two-thirds of their

500 men in the struggle, but they valiantly hung on for over three months. Ever since those days, the British have recruited soldiers from specific villages in Nepal.

Loyalty and tenacity would become the hallmark of the Gurkha. In World War I, more than 200,000 Nepalese fought for the British Empire, with the Gurkhas fighting with valor at Gallipoli and in France, Mesopotamia, and India. The Gurkhas won nine Victoria Crosses, Britain's highest military honor. Sir Ralph Turner, who served with the 3rd Queen Alexandra's Own Gurkha Rifles in World War I, would make this dedication to his Nepalese colleagues in 1931: "Bravest of the brave, most generous of the generous, never had country more faithful friends than you." The quote is inscribed on the Gurkha memorial in London.

The Gurkhas again proved vital in World War II, especially in North Africa and the East, with Tul Bahadur Pun winning a Victoria Cross for single-handedly knocking out a Japanese gun post that had been responsible for the deaths of most of his colleagues. Significant victories included Bishenpur in 1943, where a single company of the 5th Gurkha Rifles captured two hilltop positions in the face of oppressive Japanese fire, with further Victoria Medals issued as a result.

With India gaining independence from Britain in 1947, the Gurkha regiments were divided between the two countries, with four of the ten becoming the Brigade of Gurkhas in the British Army. The British regiments proved themselves in the East once more during the Malayan Emergency in the 1950s, and during operations in Indonesia and Borneo in the following decade. While stationed in Hong Kong prior to 1997, the Brigade of Gurkhas is now based in England with some troops in Brunei, but has diminished in number to 3,600 soldiers. These days Nepalese soldiers are allowed to become officers, have the same pay and pensions as other regular British Army soldiers, and have the right to continued British residency after four years of service.

As part of Operation Herrick, the Gurkhas were deployed to Afghanistan, close to their homeland, and the history of their recent service there is littered with tales of valor. One typically courageous example

Opposite: A Gurkha solider patrolling in Afghanistan, where a number of soldiers in the Brigade earned the Military Cross for their outstanding bravery

occurred on 4 November 2008 when the 2nd Royal Gurkha Rifles were sent to clear Taliban-held compounds in Musa Qala. To attack one of the compounds, they had to cross over 250 yards of exposed open ground, and immediately they came under fire.

The riflemen made themselves into difficult targets, weaving and keeping low to the ground, but Rifleman Yubraj Rai was hit. Rifleman Dhan, as reported by the Ministry of Defence, said: "Rifleman Yubraj dropped to the ground and I did the same. I thought he was taking cover. He didn't move for a while and suddenly shouted. I noticed he was hit by an enemy bullet."

Dhan crawled towards Yubraj to give assistance, while two fellow Gurkhas immediately also put their lives at risk, running to reach his prone body while heavy gunfire kicked up dust around them. "They pulled him to a safer compound and I was responding to enemy fire using both mine and Yub's weapon." After the battle, Dhan said, "I never noticed the bullets landing around me, but I was shocked when I heard from other members of the section and the platoon how close the rounds had been." The bravery of the three men enabled the medical evacuation of Yubraj Rai, but his life could not be saved.

Several other Gurkhas earned the Military Cross for their actions in Afghanistan in 2007-08. These included Lance Corporal Agnish Thapa of the Royal Gurkha Rifles, who dragged a wounded Australian SAS soldier across a hundred yards of open ground while under heavy fire. Rifleman Bhim Bahadur Gurung crossed open ground twice, with no covering fire, to carry a wounded soldier across his shoulders to the safety of a compound. Meanwhile, Lance Corporal Mohansingh Tangnami volunteered to lead a team into an area exposed to a barrage of enemy fire in order to prevent a machine gun falling into enemy hands.

The British Empire may be long gone, but a unit initiated in a foreign land centuries ago continues to perform extraordinary acts of valor in the name of the British Army.

The Green Berets

The small units of elite soldiers secreted behind enemy lines to train local resistance fighters and conduct covert operations

AIRBORNE

"I WILL NEVER surrender though I be the last. If I am taken, I pray that I may have the strength to spit upon my enemy. My goal is to succeed in any mission—and live to succeed again. I am a member of my nation's chosen soldiery. God grant that I may not be found wanting, that I will not fail this sacred trust." These words form the creed of the United States Special Forces, otherwise known as the Green Berets.

Unconventional warfare in America has a history older than the United States itself. From the ranger units used by the early British settlers to the skirmish tactics of Rogers' Rangers, on into the 20th century and beyond, there has always been a need for men willing to fight in harsh conditions, using unconventional methods to gain the upper hand in enemy territory. The US Special Forces, created in the aftermath of World War II, are the fulcrum of those centuries of experience.

Despite their history, the Special Forces have often been treated with skepticism by much of the regular army, who are suspicious of their unorthodox techniques,

FACT FILE

REGION: Worldwide

ERA: 1952–present day

KEY ENCOUNTERS: Vietnam War 1961–73, including Battle of Nam Dong 1964; Gulf War 1991; War in Afghanistan 2001

TACTICS AND TECHNIQUES: Small units that assist and train allied forces while undertaking reconnaissance missions and black ops

WEAPONRY: SPR sniper rifle; M4A1 carbine; MP5 submachine gun; M9 pistol; MK44 minigun; all-terrain vehicles; infrared target illuminators for night operations

LEGACY: Famous for infiltration into enemy-occupied territory and unconventional operations

which are sometimes matched by the soldiers' unorthodox personalities. The CIA are similarly wary of these soldiers who specialize in covert operations behind the lines in overseas territories, as the Agency regards this as its own private domain. However, the US Special Forces are an unconventional oddity that has proved essential to modern warfare, and they have gained great respect throughout the world. The green beret, the symbol of the Special Forces, is worn with immense pride and is emblematic of the bravura of these men who step beyond the norm, isolated in inhospitable conditions in foreign lands.

Above: US Special Forces attend the wreath-laying ceremony at the grave of President John F. Kennedy at Arlington National Cemetery, 2011; the assassinated president was a great supporter of the Green Berets

Above: Jean Larrieu, a Jedburgh marine, receives the Croix de Guerre avec Palme from Charles de Gaulle, 5 September 1944; American operatives worked with French agents in the Jedburgh teams to operate covertly in German-occupied France, becoming the forefathers of the Green Berets

The immediate predecessors to the Green Berets were the multinational Jedburgh teams of World War II. Fifteen-man units of specially trained soldiers, including US operators, went behind enemy lines in German-occupied France. They helped the covert French Resistance while also collecting data about German troop and armament movements. Sabotage on supply lines and communications became a specialty: the Jedburgh teams and French Resistance worked together to destroy hundreds of bridges within France, which seriously damaged German attempts to support the front in Normandy following the Allied landings on D-Day, 1944—the operation that turned the war in the Allied favor. While pursuing its aims, the 19 Jedburgh teams hidden in France killed almost a thousand German soldiers, but lost only seven men. These operatives, working for the Office of Special Services, the precursor to the CIA, helped to create the blueprint for the Green Berets: the ability to work in small covert teams in enemy territory to aid resistance and disrupt enemy activity. Independence, decision-making, physical skills and tactical acumen, as well as knowing a foreign language, would remain pivotal in the new, post-war era of Special Forces.

The Korean War again reinforced the value of unconventional units such as the Jedburgh teams. In 1952, 2,500 slots were made available for volunteers from the regular army, who underwent enhanced specialist training to become temporary Special Forces soldiers. Colonel Aaron Bank, the man most responsible for creating the Special Forces, was an admirer of the covert work of the British Commandos, who wore green berets, so the new US troops—unofficially at first—adopted the same headwear and it became the nickname of the Special Forces. When setting up the Special Warfare School at Fort Bragg in 1956 as a center to train Special Forces, Bank described their role as "to infiltrate by land, sea, or air, deep into enemy-occupied territory and organize the resistance/guerilla potential to conduct Special Forces operations with the emphasis on guerilla warfare," a summation of Green Beret activity that remains entirely accurate to this day.

In 1961, President John F. Kennedy realized the importance of the Green Berets for the conflict in Vietnam, which had become inevitable as a result of the United States' desire to control the spread of communism in Southeast Asia. The Special Forces were reorganized and enlarged. Just like the Jedburgh teams, Green Berets would operate in units of up to 15 men and would be dropped behind enemy lines, in this case in remote areas of Vietnam and Laos. They would help train and lead local resistance to the communist forces of the Viet Cong, while damaging enemy communications and supply lines.

George Perkins, a US Air Force Combat Air Controller, found himself attached to one of those Green Beret units right in the heart of the jungle in 1962, near the beginning of the Vietnam War. His experiences highlighted the daily bravery of the Green Berets and also the psychological trauma that many operators suffered during and after their covert attempts to help the

Below: US Special Forces with South Vietnamese soldiers during the Vietnam War

South Vietnamese resistance. He arrived at a Special Forces "B" Camp where Major Ernest Trevor was leading the Green Beret operation, and his role was to help call in accurate air strikes on the Viet Cong forces. Perkins, as recounted in Jon E. Lewis' *The Secrets of the SAS and Elite Forces*, recalled: "Trevor was a gung-ho Green Beret. He liked us Air Force guys but doubted we'd be much use to him. He was wrong."

On 1 November, Trevor, Perkins, and the South Vietnamese troops they were leading were ambushed by a large Viet Cong force. "Men were getting killed around us. Mortar shells careened into our midst, coughing up clods of earth and spraying shrapnel. Bursts of automatic fire whipped over my head as I snake-crawled [towards Major Trevor]." Perkins needed to call in an air strike, but the Green Berets could not fix the Viet Cong position. If they did not get the location exactly right, it was likely they would be the victims of friendly fire.

Below and opposite:
The Green Berets are divided into five active-duty groups with special skills relevant to different areas of the world, but all are highly trained in the fundamentals of modern warfare

Perkins took two Vietnamese troops and "we began hacking our way uphill ... slicing through the bush with our machetes .... Then we literally walked into three stray Cong." His military instincts kicked in. "Less than three meters apart, we exchanged gunfire. I killed two, one of my men got the third." One of his own Vietnamese soldiers was hit, but Perkins still

needed to get closer to identify the main Viet Cong position, so he continued to hack his way towards the enemy with the remaining soldier.

They soon found out exactly where the Cong were. "I hit the deck as grenades started exploding in the foliage nearby." Perkins could see that 100 Cong were firing from a row of sandbags on a ridge. Then another grenade found its target: "Shrapnel tore through my fatigues, slashing my arms, back, buttocks." Nonetheless, Perkins was able to call in the position. The strike would be very close to the point where Perkins and the South Vietnamese soldier were now attempting to find cover from a barrage of enemy fire but, if the strike didn't go ahead immediately, Perkins thought he would be cut to shreds in any case. The napalm, dropped from overhead by a squadron of T-28s, hit home and the Green Berets found the scorched corpses of 65 Cong on the ridge. Perkins survived with minor wounds, but he did not revel in the success. "We had scored what the South Vietnamese would later call a 'great victory,' but to me it was all a little sickening."

In 1964 the Military Assistance Command, Vietnam: Studies and Observations Group (MAC-SOG) was introduced; the name was a cover for the clandestine Green Beret teams that were already being sent behind enemy lines in Vietnam, Laos, and Cambodia for long periods. According to the MAC directive, the group would undertake highly classified covert operations "to execute an intensified program of harassment, diversion, political pressure, capture of prisoners, physical destruction, acquisition of intelligence, generation of propaganda, and diversion of resources, against the Democratic Republic of Vietnam."

Today, in order to ensure their effectiveness in conflicts throughout the world, the Special Forces are divided into five active-duty groups which cover different areas: Pacific and Eastern Asia; Caribbean and West Africa; Southwest Asia and Northeast Africa; Central and South America; Europe and Western Asia. The soldiers are all rigorously trained in the culture of these areas as well as in the appropriate languages. However, the enduring US Army presence in Afghanistan since 2001 meant that all the active-duty groups were deployed to that country, whatever their specialist geographical designation.

The trainees are required to have a good record in the infantry or airborne divisions. They have parachute training, as the troops are often dropped into enemy territory, and they undergo Ranger training if they have not amassed these skills while in their regular units. Additional skills such as demolition and communications are divided up within a unit. They learn at least one language common to their assigned active-duty group, for instance Arabic in the Southwest Asia and Northeast Africa Group.

The long, complicated, and ultimately unsuccessful campaign in Vietnam is widely regarded as a dark and troubled episode in US military history—and fictional films such as *Apocalypse Now!* and the *Rambo* series are teeming with tales of Special Forces veterans going off the rails. However, amongst the chaos the Green Berets have scored many notable successes. Ultimately, Vietnam would prove to have been a hard but vital training ground for future covert operations.

Green Beret-led victories included the Battle of Nam Dong in July 1964. Twelve Green Berets from Special Forces A Team 726, led by Captain Roger H.C. Donlon, plus one Australian operative, were training and organizing a local defense force of 300 South Vietnamese at Nam Dong near the border

PROJECT GAMMA

MANY GREEN BERET operations conducted during the Vietnam War remained highly classified. From April 1968, the B-57 Special Forces detachment operated under the codename Project GAMMA. The purpose of the black-ops unit was to collect intelligence on the movements of the Viet Cong and its allies in Cambodia, and to direct attacks on the enemy. GAMMA featured 50 operatives, many of whom acted alone behind enemy lines or in very small groups, often under pseudonyms with an assumed rank, and sometimes without uniform. Only the Military Assistance Command Vietnam—rather than commanding officers—and the White House knew what black ops were being conducted by the soldiers. They even carried a special identification document to protect them from interference from allied units, reading: "The person who is identified by this document is acting under the direct orders of the President of the Unites States. Do not detain or question him." Early on, GAMMA operators, who handled local agents, provided a stunning level of intelligence to the military, but insiders believed that the project had become compromised by a double agent. As a result, on 20 June 1969, three GAMMA operators were sent to "terminate with extreme prejudice" Chu Van Thai Khac, a Vietnamese agent. They interrogated him, shot him in the head, and dumped his body at sea. However, his handler Sgt. Alvin Smith feared himself the next target on the hit list and reported the execution, which led to charges against the GAMMA hitmen. The charges were dropped but the highly secretive black ops of the Special Forces were temporarily exposed to the light.

with Laos. Operations from the camp had proved a successful irritant to Viet Cong forces in the area, so at 2:30 a.m. of 6 July, the Cong launched a massive surprise attack with a force of 900 soldiers. The camp was hit by a full-scale mortar assault. The Berets, the Australian Warrant Officer, and the South Vietnamese fought off the assault for seven hours, preventing the Cong from breaching the perimeter of the camp. Donlon, who suffered shrapnel wounds, was awarded the Medal of Honor for killing two sappers who were about to breach the defenses with explosives. The Viet Cong, dispirited, were forced to abandon the assault and retreated into the jungle. The battle proved that with the help of the Green Berets, South Vietnamese villagers could score victories against the communists.

At the height of the Vietnam War, which continued until 1973, there were 100,000 Green Berets; today there are only 20,000. In the 1980s, small detachments of Green Berets trained local forces in El Salvador and other Central American countries in attempts to defeat left-wing militias. In the following decade they provided a pivotal role working with allied Arab forces during the Gulf War, and were deployed with the United Nations

Below and opposite:
Green Beret missions can involve covert incursions behind enemy lines by land, sea or air

peace-keeping force in Somalia, Africa. Time and time again, the Green Berets' combination of local languages and cultural affinity, coupled with a willingness to fight in small units in inhospitable, enemy terrain, would prove essential as the nature of warfare changed throughout the world.

Their unconventional approach and elite skills received both acclaim and media attention at the beginning of the war in Afghanistan in the fall of 2001, following the 9/11 terrorist attacks. Green Berets were the first Western forces to enter Afghanistan. Assimilation in foreign lands is key to the role of the Green Berets, so for Afghani operations they would speak the local language and grow their beards long. Disguised as Afghans and riding horses, Green Berets fought alongside the United States' Afghani allies; they proved to be an essential reconnaissance tool on the ground, enabling the US force to call in devastating airstrikes against the Taliban forces. After the close of the wars in both Iraq and Afghanistan, their training, communications, and liaison skills would continue to prove essential in attempts to rebuild the countries; Green Berets helped to train the local security forces and played a key role in development projects.

Sayeret Matkal

The Israeli counter-terrorist and special reconnaissance unit involved in the raid on Entebbe and covert operations throughout the Middle East

EVER SINCE THE State of Israel was created in 1948, it has had a difficult relationship with its Arab neighbors, leading to open warfare but also a continual undercurrent of covert activities ranging from deep reconnaissance and surveillance to insertion and extraction operations, assassinations, and raids. Israel's elite special forces unit for counter-terrorist and intelligence-gathering operations is Sayeret Matkal ("General Staff Reconnaissance Unit"), created in 1958 and inspired by the UK's Special Air Service. "The Unit," as it is simply known, has borrowed the SAS motto of "Who Dares Wins." As the unit is top secret, its operators are not allowed to wear any insignia in public.

The deeply secret elite is trained at the special forces base at Mitkan Adam. The selection phase, called "Gibush," is arduous and, like other special forces' systems, it is designed to push candidates over the edge both physically and mentally, making them perform in pressurized and sleep-deprived conditions. The SAS, Navy SEALs, and Delta Force have secretly been

FACT FILE

REGION: Middle East
ERA: 1958–present day
KEY ENCOUNTERS: Yom Kippur War 1973; Ma'a lot Massacre 1974; Operation Thunderbolt 1976; Operation Orchid 2007
TACTICS AND TECHNIQUES: Covert unit for deep reconnaissance, anti-terrorist activities, and hostage situations
WEAPONRY: Uzi and small arms
LEGACY: Conducted one of history's most acclaimed special operations at Entebbe airport

involved in the training of Sayeret Matkal recruits in a year-and-a-half long program, known as "Maslul." The comprehensive program includes hostage rescue, combat shooting and sniping, close-quarter battle techniques, navigation and reconnaissance, assassination, explosives, and survival skills. Soldiers are also taught specialist parachuting such as HALO (high altitude, low opening), heliborne insertion and extraction, and combat swimming.

Sayeret Matkal answers directly to the Israel Defense Forces' High Command. Its elite training regime was stepped up and its counter-terrorist purpose further emphasized after the murder of Israeli athletes at the Munich Olympics of 1972 and the hostage disaster at Ma'alot High School in 1974. At Ma'alot, a Sayeret Matkal sniper failed to perform

Below: Entebbe airport, scene of Operation Thunderbolt in 1974, when a Sayeret Matkal team assaulted the airport building to free over 100 hostages

a clean hit on a terrorist, who consequently began throwing grenades and mowing down hostages. In the unit's assault, 25 hostages died, including 21 children, and it was responsible for two deaths caused by friendly fire. As a result, a different unit, Yamam, was created as a domestic counter-terrorist unit, while Sayeret Matkal became a specialized commando unit for covert operations on foreign soil, where stealth is key. It has two teams ready for action overseas at all times.

The overhaul was almost immediately effective. In 1976, Sayeret Matkal was acclaimed for its part in Operation Thunderbolt, one of the most notable operations in the history of counter-terrorism. On 27 June, the Popular Front for the Liberation of Palestine hijacked an Air France flight from Tel Aviv to Paris, via Athens. The hijackers diverted the plane to Libya and then to Entebbe airport in Uganda, whose leader Idi Amin supported their cause. Non-Israeli passengers were released, with the hijackers holding the crew and the remaining hostages, totaling 106 people, in the airport terminal. They threatened to kill the hostages if their demands for the release of 40 Palestinian prisoners held in Israel, along with 13 prisoners incarcerated in other countries, were not met.

Mossad, the Israeli secret service, carefully gathered intelligence prior to the rescue mission, Operation Thunderbolt, on 4 July. Four Hercules aircraft landed at Entebbe airport at night without detection by Ugandan air control. The planes housed a 29-man Sayeret Matkal team that would conduct the assault on the building; paratroopers who would secure the airfield; Sayeret Golani soldiers who would transfer the hostages to one of the Hercules; and other Sayeret Matkal operators who would blow up the Ugandan Air Force's MiG-17 and MiG-21 aircraft to stop them interfering with the extraction operation.

The operation lasted just 90 minutes, in which the commandos stormed the building, killed seven hijackers and 45 Ugandan soldiers, successfully extracted almost all the hostages onto a plane while under fire, and destroyed up to 30 Ugandan aircraft. Three hostages were killed along with the Sayeret Matkal unit commander, Yonatan Netanyahu, the older brother of future Israeli Prime Minister Benjamin Netanyahu (who also served in Sayeret Matkal). Considering the situation—a long-range mission to deal with a mass hostage situation in an enemy country—the operation was deemed a stunning success.

Israeli Defense Forces refuse to provide information about the activities of Sayeret Matkal, but it is believed to be conducting an ongoing campaign of kidnappings, assassinations, and sabotage in Arab states. Its commandos are thought to have secretly invaded the site of a nuclear reactor in Syria in Operation Orchid, September 2007, and put in place the laser designators that guided the missiles which destroyed the plant.

Sayeret Matkal has been accused of acting like other historical elites, sometimes pursuing its own interests, and using its position as an elite force to exert undue influence in the political sphere. In 2003, 13 unit reservists were charged with trying to abuse the political prestige of the unit when they presented a letter to the prime minister, Ariel Sharon: "We say to you today, we will no longer give our hands to the oppressive reign in the [Arab-occupied] territories and the denial of human rights to millions of Palestinians, and we shall no longer serve as the defensive shield for the settlement campaign." The men were expelled from the ranks and their attempt to align the Sayeret Matkal to supporters of liberal policy in the region failed.

Navy SEALs

The covert US commando, demolition, and surgical strike teams, often linked to the CIA

"IT'S A WEIRD FEELING, watching yourself being prepared to die. It was like they expected me to go along with my own murder, to be a good victim and not say a word," Captain Richard Phillips wrote in his memoir, *A Captain's Duty.* Somali pirates had captured Phillips' container ship, the Maersk Alabama, on 8 April 2009. Their speedboat had been disabled but the pirates took Phillips hostage and left the ship by lifeboat. On Friday 10 April a team of Navy SEAL snipers, who had flown non-stop from Virginia, parachuted into nearby waters to join the crew of USS *Bainbridge*, which agreed to tow the lifeboat while negotiations continued.

Phillips thought he was about to be executed following an escape attempt and was struggling with the hostage-takers. "I thought in the back of my mind, *How long can you keep this up?* Not long, I knew. *Better say your goodbyes.*" He thought it was the end. "All of a sudden there was an explosion near my left ear ... I felt blood spurting out between my fingers and running down my face. *Holy shit, he really did it*, I thought. *He shot me.*" He had been struck but it wasn't his time to die as the pirates argued over whether to execute him or not.

FACT FILE

REGION: Worldwide
ERA: 1962–present day
KEY ENCOUNTERS: Vietnam War 1962–70; Grenada 1983; Panama 1989; Afghanistan from 2001; Iraq from 2003; Operation Neptune Spear 2011
TACTICS AND TECHNIQUES: Covert unit for deep penetration behind enemy lines, anti-terrorist activities, and surgical raids
WEAPONRY: HK416 and M4 carbines; HK MP7A1 submachine gun; SIG-Sauer P226 pistol; sniper rifles
LEGACY: Elite commandos famous for killing Osama bin Laden

On Sunday 12 April, the Navy SEALs would see one of the Somalis getting ready to pull the trigger of his AK-47 and shoot Captain Phillips in the back. Commander Frank Castellano on the *Bainbridge* gave the order to fire and the SEAL snipers—perhaps the most expert marksmen in the entire American armed services—killed the three Somali pirates in the lifeboat with single shots to the head. Phillips was finally safe. The captain would later say of his saviors: "They're the titans. They're impossible men doing an impossible job, and they did the impossible with me ... They're at the point of the sword every day."

Those US Navy snipers were from the Special Warfare Development Group, called DEVGRU for short, the elite force formerly known as SEAL Team 6. Two years later, the same SEAL unit dispatched Osama bin Laden in a compound in Pakistan.

Above: A landing craft approaches Omaha Beach, on D-Day 1944, after the way had been partially cleared by Underwater Demolition Teams, the forerunners of the Navy SEALs

Above: The insignia of the Navy Seals

Below: US soldiers reach Utah Beach on D-Day, 1944

The Navy SEALs were created in 1962, but the organization was a direct descendant of the Underwater Demolition Teams (UDTs), which had been formed 20 years earlier during World War II. With the prospect of needing to land large-scale Allied forces on the beaches of enemy-occupied territory, the US had developed small teams of specialists who could conduct the reconnaissance of possible landing sites. Equipped with small inflatable boats and underwater breathing apparatus, they would silently slip ashore to analyze terrain and gather intelligence on enemy positions prior to a major landing. Both onshore and underwater, they used small explosives to demolish any obstacles that would hinder boats or landing craft. As well as being experts in explosives, sailing and swimming, these stealthy UDT operators were proficient in close quarter battle and small-arms fire, in case their covert operations met with detection.

The Underwater Demolition Teams, which began their specialist training in 1942 at the Amphibious Training Base at Little Creek, Virginia, comprised volunteers from both the army and navy. They were formed into companies of 80 men, usually with 16 officers, and each company was broken up into mini assault teams. Their first major mission was in preparation for the US landing at the Japanese-occupied Kwajalein Atoll in the Marshall Islands of the Pacific, in January 1944. The resultant US victory was a significant blow to the Japanese: their defenses had been breached for the first time. The UDTs' success in that mission meant that demolition teams would go on to be deployed prior to all major US landings in the Pacific theater for the rest of World War II.

The UDTs were also used on the shores of France for the D-Day landings in Normandy, June 1944. They sabotaged German obstacles aimed at stopping landings on what became known as Omaha and Utah beaches. The 175 men who were sent to clear Omaha took heavy casualties, with 31 killed and 60 wounded, but managed to demolish enough obstacles to create around a dozen clear entry lanes for landing craft. Back in the East, the UDTs prepared the beachhead for the huge landing at Okinawa in April 1945. Most of the demolition teams were disbanded at the close of World War II but they were revived in the Korean War of 1950–53, where their role was broadened to include sabotage further inland, with the teams stealing ashore at night to hit transport links, such as railway lines and tunnels, and communications.

Above: Navy SEALs specialize in covert amphibious attacks but are trained to face all conditions at land or sea

On 1 January 1962 the UDTs evolved into a commando unit with full airborne, amphibious, and land-fighting skills, and were re-designated as Sea, Air, and Land Teams, leading to the acronym SEALs. Despite their training for parachuting and land roles, they remained part of the US Navy.

They have become one of the best commando elites in the world, with a selection and training regime equally as tough as those of US Delta Force and the British Special Air Service. The successful volunteers undergo more than a year of intensive training involving scuba diving, parachuting, demolitions, boat handling, climbing, and abseiling, and they are impressive marksmen. Their missions are both coastal and inland, involving surgical raids into enemy territory, sabotage, covert intelligence gathering, and dealing with hostage situations. The SEAL code includes the mantra: "Ready to lead. Ready to follow. Never quit ... Excel as warriors through discipline and innovation. Train for war. Fight to win. Defeat our nation's enemies." The unit's insignia is a winged trident, crossed with an anchor and a rifle. The SEAL code concludes: "Earn your Trident every day," while the unit's motto is "The only easy day was yesterday."

Immediately after the SEALs were created, they were deployed to Vietnam, where they would undertake covert operations throughout the Southeast Asian conflict up to 1970. Like the Green Berets, they had a training role, teaching the commandos of the South Vietnamese Navy, but they were continually active as anti-guerilla units conducting raids and ambushes in the Viet Cong-occupied Mekong Delta. They specialized in using small vessels to navigate the network of waterways and launch night-time attacks. The Vietnam War was a difficult, extended episode in US military history, but the SEALs emerged with a much enhanced reputation.

Control of the SEALs was later shifted to the Joint Special Operations Command (under the broad control of the United States Special Operations Command), and their role is sometimes orchestrated in tandem with the Green Berets, Rangers, and Delta Force. The unit now has over a thousand members, split up into teams, which are again divided up into three 40-man units comprising smaller squads. As well as undertaking discrete missions, the Seals accompany the US Navy fleets, and are involved in a wide range of unconventional operations on land and sea, training the commandos of allied forces, fighting pirates threatening US vessels (especially off the coast of Somalia), and tracking and killing terrorist leaders in the Middle East.

Opposite: A Navy SEAL carrying an M4 carbine

Opposite: Navy SEALs have been deployed in special operations in South America, Somalia, Iraq and Afghanistan

SEAL Team 6, an elite within the elite fighting force, was set up in November 1980. Sometimes known as "The Mob," Team 6 was created as a counter-terrorist unit designed to act against threats to US shipping and oil rigs, and likewise to conduct assaults on enemy ships and rigs, as well as to provide operational support to Delta Force. They were involved in Operation Urgent Fury in Grenada in 1983; the *Achille Lauro* hijacking situation of 1985, in which the Palestinian Liberation Front took control of a civilian ship off the coast of Egypt; and the invasion of Panama in 1989. In the latter, SEAL Teams 2, 4, and 6 undertook a variety of missions including the seizure of Paitilla airport and the destruction of Panamanian dictator General Manuel Noriega's plane. Meanwhile, in an old-style commando raid, SEALs swam underwater into Balboa Harbor to attach C4 explosives to the hull of Noriega's gunboat, blowing it up.

Since 1987, SEAL Team 6 has been renamed the United States Special Warfare Development Group, but they are still known informally by their original name. The US Navy refuses to comment on its operations or even its existence, so its official directive remains secret, but there can be little doubt that since then the team has been further developed to specialize in the most extreme counter-insurgency operations and assassinations. The CIA's Special Activities Division is known to recruit operators from the Navy SEALs, and especially DEVGRU, for its elite Special Operations Group.

In October 1993, a small unit of snipers from Navy SEAL Team 6 was involved in the Battle of Mogadishu, otherwise known as "Black Hawk Down," in Somalia. The snipers had been in the country since August 1993 on a mission to track down and execute Mohammed Farrah Aidid, a Somali warlord. The unit took part in a US special operations and CIA raid against Somali militia at the Olympic Hotel in Mogadishu, the country's capital city, but the operation turned into a catastrophe when two of the force's Black Hawk helicopters were downed. The raiding force was trapped and incurred casualties before a successful rescue operation could intervene. Hundreds (or thousands according to some reports) of guerillas were killed or wounded, but the much-publicized operation besmirched the reputation of US special operations forces.

However, the four SEAL snipers performed with excellence, each earning the Silver Star for their bravery. Navy SEAL Howard E. Wasdin was wounded three times during the battle, but fought on, earning himself a Purple

US MARINES FORCE CORPS RECONNAISSANCE

LIKE THE NAVY SEALS, the US Marines Corps Force Reconnaissance (Force Recon) specializes in amphibious operations, surgical insertion and extraction behind enemy lines, and demolition. Since the creation of the Marine Special Operations Teams in 2007, it is less involved in direct action, and more concerned with deep reconnaissance in enemy-occupied territory. Deep reconnaissance missions are classed as "green ops," distinct from the "black ops" of direct action. Force Recon, created in 1957 but with ancestral units operational in World War II, conducted both types of operations in Vietnam. In recent decades it has had a role in Operation Desert Storm (1991), Operation Enduring Freedom (from 2001 onwards), and Operation Iraqi Freedom (2003–11). Its black ops force, renamed the Marine Special Operations Teams, is now controlled by the Marine Corps Forces Special Operations Command, a component of the United States Special Operations Command, which oversees and coordinates combined operations by all the armed services.

Heart. Captain Eric T. Olson was also amongst the SEAL combatants, and was cited for his actions in the battle: "while under withering enemy fire ... Captain Olson demonstrated a complete disregard for his own personal safety in the accomplishment of his mission." The overall operation may have been a failure, but the Team 6 shooters' activities enhanced the SEALs' almost peerless reputation for performing with military excellence during unconventional operations in extremely dangerous situations. Olson became the commanding officer of DEVGRU just a year later, in 1994.

Following the Islamic terrorist attacks against the United States of 11 September 2001, one of the main focal points of SEAL operations has been the Middle East. SEAL teams went behind enemy lines in both Afghanistan and Iraq prior to the invasions to conduct reconnaissance missions. Following the end of the wars, SEALs continued to undertake operations in the hinterlands of both countries, with the principal task of tracking and neutralizing the leaders of al-Qaeda and other terrorist groups.

Mark Owen (a pseudonym) was the team leader of the hand-picked unit of 24 men in SEAL Team 6 that conducted Operation Neptune Spear—the raid on Osama bin Laden's compound in Abbottabad, Pakistan—on 1 May 2011. President Barrack Obama gave the go-ahead for the operation, but no foreign officials in Pakistan or any allied secret services were notified: like all of

Right: Members of a SEAL team practice desert combat techniques. SEAL teams have to be capable of performing rapid strikes in any terrain

Team 6's operations, this was a top secret mission. As former SEAL Howard Wasdin described in his book *SEAL Team Six*, during the operation, "Wearing night-vision goggles, each SEAL carried an M4 rifle and a SIG-Sauer 9mm pistol on his hip as a backup." They were meant to abseil into the compound from a Black Hawk, but the helicopter could not stabilize for the drop so they were forced to hit the ground and assault the compound from the exterior.

At 01:00, according to Wasdin, "Blasting through doors, they clear left and right, rounding up whoever they can." Mark Owen and his team went up to the third floor of the compound, where they found bin Laden, the al-Qaeda leader who had initiated the 9/11 attacks of 2001 and had evaded capture ever since. Reportedly, bin Laden did not surrender and took bullets to the head and chest in the Team 6 execution.

The operation confirmed that DEVGRU is not just the most elite SEAL team, but one of the most impressive covert fighting bodies in the world. Mark Owen concluded in his memoir, *No Easy Day*: "We are not superheroes, but we all share a common bond in serving something greater than ourselves. It is a brotherhood that ties us together. And that bond is what allows us to willingly walk into harm's way together."

Above: Navy SEALs demonstrate the rapid insertion and extraction skills used during Operation Neptune Spear

Alpha Group

The mysterious counter-terrorism and covert operations task force of the Russian Federal Security Service

OPERATION STORM-333, 27 December 1979: A select team of 24 of the Soviet Union security service's most elite fighters stormed the presidential palace in Kabul, Afghanistan. Their mission: to kill the President. In just 43 minutes they would have achieved their aim, slaying hundreds of Afghan soldiers, toppling the Afghan government in a bloodbath, and setting up a new regime. The fighters were from Directorate A, otherwise known as Spetsgruppa A or Alpha Group, the mysterious elite task force set up by the Soviet Union's KGB. The unit had only been in existence for five years, having been formed in response to the Munich massacre in 1972, where members of the Israeli Olympic team were killed by Palestinian terrorists. Yuri Andropov, the KGB head who would become leader of the Soviet Union, wanted a team that could specialize in hit-and-run counter-terrorism missions, assassinations, and covert operations on foreign soil.

The Russian special forces are so secretive that most trainees—always the very best available conscripts—have little idea what Spetsnaz ("special purpose

Opposite: Tajbeg Palace in Kabul, stormed by Alpha Group in Operation Storm-333 in an operation to remove the Afghan president in 1979

FACT FILE

REGION: Former Soviet Union, Afghanistan, Lebanon
ERA: 1974–present day
KEY ENCOUNTERS: Operation Storm-333 1979; Battle of Grozny 1996; Moscow theatre crisis 2002; Beslan crisis 2004
TACTICS AND TECHNIQUES: Rapid assault team used for covert operations and hostage crises
WEAPONRY: PP-19 Bizon submachine gun, sniper rifles, AK-9 assault rifle, grenades, smoke bombs, flamethrowers
LEGACY: The leading Russian special operations force, feared for its brutality

force") is when they join, but Alpha is another step up in both secrecy and elitism. Alpha now has about 300 operatives, trained in counter-sabotage, airborne, mountain, and amphibious assault skills. Sergei Goncharov of the Alpha veterans association explains what happens to the new recruits: "They go through it all—the physical and psychological training, breaking down fear barriers, learning to shoot anything that can shoot and drive anything that could be driven. It's incredibly tough. Many break along the way and leave." Those that survive the rigorous training become elite fighters, trained to storm buildings, battle terrorists, and put their lives on the line to protect Mother Russia.

The unit has always been shrouded in secrecy, but Alpha officer Oleg Balashov gave an insight into one of its most acclaimed missions, Operation Storm-333, conducted in December 1979: "Our first op was seizing the Afghan leader's palace in Kabul. I had no idea where we were going, but we knew it wasn't a drill. By the time we got to Afghanistan, we figured it out. On the ground, we met some fellow commandos who told us they had brought the future Afghan government." The existing communist government in Afghanistan was about to be swept aside in a hail of bullets.

The KGB had believed that Hafizullah Amin, the President of Afghanistan, was a possible CIA agent colluding with Pakistan and China in plots against the Soviet Union. They decided that it was time to replace him with a Soviet puppet president.

The covert team was led by 24 agents of the "Thunder" detachment of Alpha, assisted by 30 agents from the equally mysterious Directorate B (also known as "Vympel"), a few paratroopers, and a large support team from the 154th Separate Spetsnaz Detachment. The latter was known as the Muslim Battalion as it was comprised of specialist soldiers from the southern Soviet republics; these men wore civilian clothes to blend in with Afghan locals. Rustam-Khadzha Tursunkulov of the Muslim Battalion recalled: "We were told that [President Amin] had been a bloody dictator responsible for the deaths of thousands of people. We had to overthrow the bloody regime and back up the Afghan people to come to power." They would provide cover for the special forces as they assaulted the palace, especially vital if the operation went wrong.

And the operation nearly did go wrong. The Afghan forces knew they were coming: "We received information that tonight something would happen. Amin called all of his commanders to the Palace as he wanted to be prepared to command all his troops against the Russians," reported Mohammed Akbar of the Afghan Army.

Before the attack, Balashov took a covert look at the palace and its surroundings while disguised as the bodyguard of a Soviet diplomat. He did not fancy his team's chances of surviving the assault on the heavily guarded Palace: they would be walking into a death trap.

Alpha Group, wearing Afghan uniforms and bulletproof vests, hit Tajbeg Palace in a rapid raid. Balashov, who was second-in-command, explained: "In each vehicle, we had four to five Alpha officers, the crew of the vehicle: the commander, the driver, and the gunner. And in addition to that, we had Afghans riding with us. In my car we had the future Afghan Defense Minister. I assigned one of my men to look after him. I told him: guard this man with your life. No matter what happens, he must stay alive."

The convoy was attacked as soon as it approached the palace, with all five troops in the lead vehicle surviving direct hits as they stormed the grounds. "To understand this massacre you have to have seen it," Balashov said. "We were shooting to protect our fighters because the gunfire was terrible. The

Above: Hafizullah Amin, the President of Afghanistan, was killed during the Alpha Group raid in December 1979

Above: The "Tree of Grief" monument to those who lost their lives in the Beslan school massacre in 2004, when 300 hostages were killed

enemy was shooting from the roof, from the windows, and they were protected by the walls while our fighters were on open ground and could be easily shot down. What I still remember and what impressed me was the number of soldiers defending the palace." There were up to 300 Afghans from the President's personal guard firing at the lead team of 24 Alpha operatives. In the ensuing battle, almost every member of the Alpha team was hit, including Balashov, but the bulletproof vests did their job: the Afghan's submachine guns were unable to penetrate the body armor. The operation's commander was killed by friendly fire, however: Alpha were fooled by his disguise and mistook him for a palace guard.

The team soon found the President, whom Mohammed Akbar claimed was already ill: "The Russians had already recruited a cook who put poison in the food. Amin was still alive when the Russian special troops got to him. Later, when we came here, we couldn't find any of his remains."

Vasili Mitrokhin, a KGB major who defected to the UK, claimed that "over a hundred of the KGB troops were killed before the palace was taken and Amin gunned down." However, this figure probably includes the many wounded, as a more reliable source states that just two of the Alpha team, three of the Vympel team, nine paratroopers, and six soldiers in the Muslim Battalion were killed. They had slain up to 200 Afghan fighters in the raid.

Babrak Karmal, the Soviet Union's preferred leader, was immediately installed as the new President of Afghanistan. Operation Storm-333 had been an incredible success for the elite force, but Afghanistan would be an unhappy battleground for the Soviets. The assassination of the President was followed by the torturous, nine-year-long Soviet-Afghan war, which led to the eventual withdrawal of Soviet troops.

Left: Alpha Group members receiving congratulations from Vladimir Putin; it is widely believed that Alpha was covertly active in Ukraine prior to the annexation of Crimea in 2014

Directorate A, however, had proved itself a fearless, highly skilled elite unit. Its ruthlessness and unorthodox approach came to the fore in 1985 when Russian diplomats were taken hostage in Beirut, Lebanon. Alpha identified the kidnappers and took their relatives hostage. Allegedly, their body parts were then sent to the hostage-takers to make it clear that there would be no negotiation, just brutal recrimination: the diplomats were released.

In 1991, Alpha held the future of Russia in its hands when it was involved in a Soviet *coup d'état* against President Boris Yeltsin. Alpha could have secured the Russian White House in half an hour, but the KGB backed out of the plan, fearing a popular uprising and immense bloodshed, and chose not to stand in the way of the dismantling of the Soviet Union and democratization of Russia. Following the demise of the KGB, Alpha became the tool of its successor, the Federal Security Service of the Russian Federation (FSB).

In post-Soviet Russia, Alpha played an important role in the wars in Chechnya and related terrorist attacks, including the hostage crises in a Moscow theatre in 2002 and at a school in Beslan in 2004, where more than 300 hostages were killed. Although the former was a success, Alpha and Vympel were both criticized for their heavy-handed assault, involving flamethrowers, at Beslan. Alpha remains feared and respected for its unflinching desire to destroy the enemy—at all costs.

Delta Force

The US detachment specializing in covert action, raids, counter terrorism, and hostage rescues in overseas lands

THE 1ST OPERATIONAL Special Forces Detachment-Delta—Delta Force—is the extremely secretive counter-terrorism unit of the United States Joint Special Operations Command. It often works in tandem with the Naval Special Warfare Development Group, usually referred to as Navy SEAL Team 6, in clandestine operations—including surgical strikes, hostage situations, and raids. Delta Force remains one of the most secretive organizations in the world, not least because the US government and the Pentagon refuse to comment publicly about its activities. However, Delta's first commanding officer Charles Beckwith and Delta operator Eric Haney have written autobiographical works that provide some insight into this elite special force.

Delta Force was set up by US Army Colonel Charlie A. Beckwith in 1977, partly in response to the hostage taking and killing of Israeli athletes at the Munich Olympics in 1972. The episode opened American eyes to the need for a specially trained super-elite unit that could deal specifically with terrorist threats and hostage situations, particularly overseas. The unit brief was more specific than that of the general Special Forces, and was originated to deal with

FACT FILE

REGION: Worldwide

ERA: 1977–present day

KEY ENCOUNTERS: Operation Eagle Claw 1980; Gulf War 1991; Afghanistan 2001; Iraq 2003

TACTICS AND TECHNIQUES: Covert unit for deep penetration behind enemy lines, anti-terrorist activities, and surgical raids

WEAPONRY: HK416 carbine; HK MP5 submachine gun; M16 rifles; sniper rifles; undisclosed special weapons developments

LEGACY: An elite with a growing reputation that performs US special operations

specific scenarios that require covert rapid action, specialist explosives and intrusion skills, supreme marksmanship, and close-combat proficiency, sometimes in far-flung, distant locations, and behind enemy lines.

Beckwith, who was drafted by the Green Bay Packers football team before choosing a career in the US Army, was a product of the Ranger School who joined the Special Forces and saw action throughout the Vietnam War. However, it was his year spent with the UK's Special Air Service (SAS) in 1962 which would provide him with the model for Delta Force. Chargin' Charlie, as Beckwith was known, was impressed by the extreme training

methods of the SAS, and its ability to work in small teams covertly and independently in overseas territories, often behind enemy lines. He recalled in *Delta Force*, his memoir, "The troops resembled no military organization I had ever known ... Everything I'd been taught about soldiering, been trained to believe, was turned upside down."

Above: Colonel Charles Beckwith, who set up Delta Force in response to the Munich Olympics massacre of 1974

The first full SAS training exercise Beckwith witnessed involved testing the soldiers' navigation skills by just giving them a compass and a very sketchy map. It then dawned on him that in order to complete the exercise by the deadline, the soldiers would have to run throughout the night, crossing rivers on the route, with virtually no rations and while carrying heavy Bergen rucksacks as well as their personal weaponry. He had never seen anything like it in a training situation. The SAS weren't being endlessly drilled on a parade ground: they were being trained to fight covertly and conduct surgical hit-and-run raids behind enemy lines in tiny four-man units ready to perform in any given situation. They were being trained for the unconventional warfare of the future.

On his return to the United States, Beckwith repeatedly resubmitted a plan to have that sort of elite force in the US, but the suggestion was turned down again and again. It was only after the Munich hostage episode that the upper echelons of the military establishment finally started to realize that Beckwith's proposal for a secret, unconventional force needed to be given the green light.

Above: Signage for Fort Bragg in North Carolina, home to Delta Force

Delta Force was created in 1977 on the SAS model of three squadrons, each of which is comprised of three smaller troops of reconnaissance, assault, and sniper specialists. These troops are divided up again into four-man units—tiny, self-sufficient teams that could work covertly in the field, thereby allowing for maximum flexibility during operations. Delta Force also has a signals squadron and an aviation platoon, which uses aircraft disguised with civilian livery and false identification markings. The detachment has its own intelligence team, sometimes referred to as the "Funny Platoon" (which includes female operatives); this is sent to infiltrate an area, and undertake reconnaissance and intelligence-gathering missions before an operation gets underway. Delta Force is further augmented by a technological unit, which specializes in eavesdropping on enemy positions and monitoring data exchanges. Delta Force has remained small, with only 200 to 300 combat operatives supported by a logistics team of approximately 2,000.

The force is based at Fort Bragg alongside the Green Berets from whom many of its recruits are drawn, with the Rangers also contributing a significant number. Like the SAS, Delta Force aims to recruit only the best, toughest, and most versatile soldiers, so the selection regime is extreme. Command Sergeant Major Eric L. Haney, who was in Delta Force from its early years until 1986, gave a detailed insight into the detachment's recruitment and training methods in his memoir, *Inside Delta Force*. The

Above: A US helicopter destroyed in Operation Eagle Claw in 1980; the disastrous Delta Force operation led to structural and procedural changes in the US Special Forces

similarities to SAS selection trials are noticeable, not least the series of longer and longer marches that need to be conducted in less and less time, finishing with a 40-mile march over difficult terrain while wearing a 45-pound rucksack and carrying equipment. The soldiers do not know how long they have to complete the course, but one second over the allotted time will mean failure. The physical testing is followed by exhausting psychological testing including interrogation simulations.

Successful recruits, who usually number only about 10 per cent of the volunteers, then attend a full counter-terrorism course, and train in parachuting, weapons proficiency, and specialties such as explosives. Like the SAS, Delta specializes in HALO (high altitude, low opening) parachute jumps, as well as using a "high altitude, high opening" technique with arms lowered to the side to prevent numbness—which could prove a killer if a soldier needs to defend himself as soon as he hits the ground. Similar to the SAS's "Killing House," Delta Force has "The House of Horrors," where operatives practice building raids and hostage-rescue missions.

Delta Force operators rarely wear a uniform, even at Fort Bragg, and when they do, it has no regimental markings. As well as civilian clothes, the operatives are allowed facial hair and longer hair than a regular trooper, all of which adds to the disguise. The effect is a far cry from that of a standard uniformed trooper with a buzz-cut.

The first recruits to Delta Force were called into action soon after the unit had become fully operational: they were not going to start life with a small-scale incursion, but one of the most audacious operations ever attempted

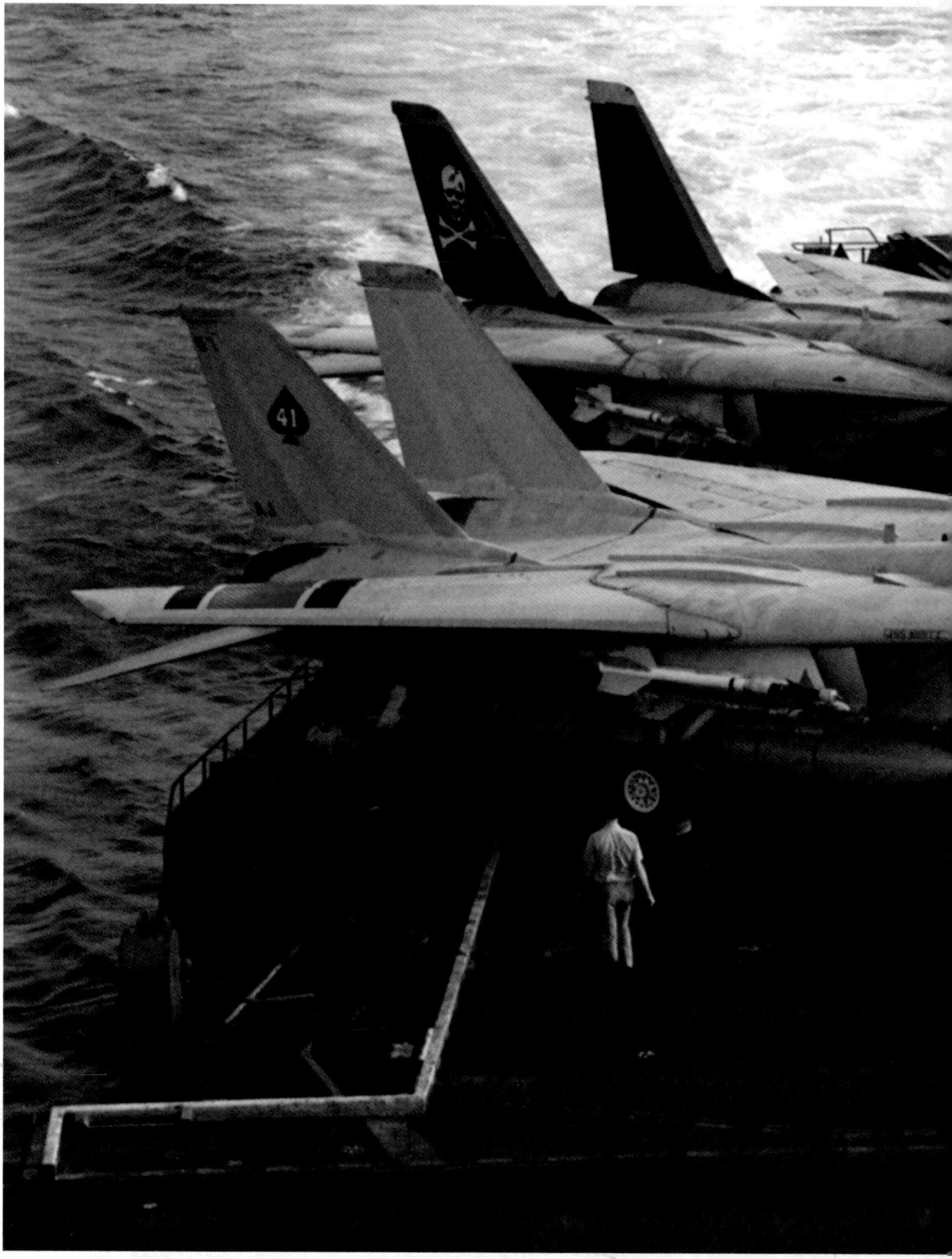
41

Left: The deck of the
USS *Nimitz* with two US
Navy Grumman F-14A
Tomcats fighter aircraft
deployed with special
markings for Operation
Eagle Claw, 1980

Above: A Sikorsky
helicopter in flight, 1987

by a special operations elite. On 4 November 1979, 52 American citizens
were taken hostage by the Iranian Revolutionary Guard in the US Embassy in
the Iranian capital of Tehran. Iran had just undergone an Islamic revolution
and now regarded the United States as an enemy. All diplomatic efforts to
release the hostages were rebuffed over the course of the next six months,
and Colonel Beckwith was finally called in to deploy his Delta Force in a major
hostage-extraction operation named Eagle Claw.

Before the operation Beckwith was called into a meeting with President
Jimmy Carter in the White House. "I was worried about what I was wearing,"
recalled Beckwith, but then he bumped into an old SAS friend in the Pentagon:
"He was wearing his SAS regimental tie and gave it to me to wear that evening.
I wanted it for good luck."

Perhaps Beckwith had forgotten that good luck was in short supply when
the SAS mounted its own first mission back in 1941. That operation was a

disaster, with two-thirds of the team captured or killed after their planes were blown off course and the troops parachuted straight into a storm, landing far from their proposed target area. Similarly weather and insufficient air support were to play a significant role in the debacle of Operation Eagle Claw.

Beckwith laid out the plan before the President, explaining that the Force would first fly by night to a remote desert spot in Iran, christened Desert One, then the operators themselves would be flown by eight of the US Marines' Sikorsky RH-53D Sea Stallion helicopters to a hideout area, Desert Two, just 50 miles outside Tehran. There, both the men and helicopters would remain concealed under camouflage material during daylight hours. At sunset, six Mercedes trucks and two small vehicles, arranged by the CIA in Tehran, would arrive to transport Delta to the capital. "Once the trucks arrived at the east wall [of the embassy] Delta Force would climb over it. Then a high-explosive charge would be placed to blow a hole in the wall large enough for an 18-wheeler to be driven through it," Beckwith explained.

Beckwith then gave detailed information about the raid, in which two units of forty men would rescue the hostages and neutralize the guards at the embassy. Meanwhile, a third unit would take control of the adjacent soccer stadium. The hostages would be taken through the hole in the perimeter to the stadium, with covering fire provided by two M60s and an HK21 machine gun. The hostages and rescue team would then be airlifted out of the stadium by the helicopters, flown to an airfield at Manzariyeh, which was to be secured by the Rangers, and air-evac'd out of the country.

THE BENGHAZI ATTACK

UP TO 150 gunmen assaulted the US diplomatic offices in Benghazi, Libya, on 11 September 2012: the date was no coincidence as the attackers were armed Islamist militants who reveled in the memory of the 9/11 terrorist attacks of 2001. The US ambassador J. Christopher Stevens and another diplomat were killed, and the machine gun and mortar fire was transferred to a CIA annex nearby. The CIA held off the attack until morning, while two Delta Force operators, five CIA agents, and Glen Doherty, an ex-Navy SEAL on the embassy security team, took over a jet in Tripoli and forced the pilots to fly to Benghazi so they could aid their colleagues. They made it into the annex before another major assault commenced. Up to 100 attackers were killed, but Doherty and another ex-SEAL, Tyrone Woods, were killed by mortar fire while manning an MK46 on the roof. A Delta operator used a handheld device to monitor the attack through images transmitted from a drone in the skies above. He reported: "There's a large element assembling, and we need to get everyone out of here now!" Almost thirty Americans were evacuated under gunfire and made it to the airport.

Beckwith was deeply concerned about the lack of immediate tactical air support for the operation, including at Manzariyeh: "I was confused ... It didn't make any sense to go through the entire raid only to get wiped out at the end by an Iranian jet jockey who happened to get lucky and knock down a C-141 carrying hostages and rescuers." Consequently, Beckwith was guaranteed aerial support for the evacuation, but other problems with air support would let down the colonel long before the operation ever reached that stage.

When flying to Desert One, one of the Sea Stallions was abandoned because the crew thought they had a cracked rotor blade. The other choppers then hit a dust storm, causing another Sea Stallion to malfunction and limp back to its aircraft carrier. The remaining helicopters had to wait for the storm to clear before they could land, putting the operation in jeopardy due to the delays to the precisely planned schedule. Then another disaster struck: a third helicopter malfunctioned, meaning that there would be too few helicopters to undertake the operation. The operation was abandoned, but not without further farce. A helicopter, kicking up its own dust storm on take-off, crashed into an EC-130 plane and both ignited, taking five lives. Wrecked American hardware was dotted over the Iranian desert without Delta Force ever managing to get anywhere near Tehran. The disaster certainly contributed to Carter losing the 1980 presidential election to Ronald Reagan.

If it had succeeded, Operation Eagle Claw would have been one of the boldest operations in the history of special operations, but it only managed to damage the reputation of the nascent Delta Force, even if insiders knew that the failure had little to do with the training and bravery of the operators.

Just like the SAS, Delta Force needed to find its feet. That first aborted mission taught a lesson to the whole special operations command structure. The 160th Special Operations Aviation Regiment was created to act as a highly trained unit to assist special operations, and the new Joint Special Operations Command was created on Beckwith's recommendation.

The new command structure and trained air support enabled Delta Force to become one of the most respected elites in the world over the course of the next 30 years. Much of its activities remain completely shielded from the public eye, but it was instrumental in pursuing US foreign policy in Central and South America in the 1980s. In the Gulf War in 1991, Delta Force worked alongside the SAS to hunt down Iraqi SCUD missile bases. From 2001

onward the elite force was heavily involved in tracking down key members of al-Qaeda and the Taliban in Afghanistan and Pakistan.

Delta Force operators are believed to have worked undercover in Baghdad prior to the invasion of Iraq in 2003. They eavesdropped on Iraqi military communications and provided intelligence to guide US airstrikes. Operators were then involved in the capture of Saddam Hussein and also guided the bomb strike that killed the al-Qaeda leader al-Zarqawi in 2006.

Eric Haney, who took part in the doomed Tehran operation, stayed with Delta's B Squadron for another six years, during which time it continually proved itself in daring clandestine operations. He prized a photo of the squadron taken in 1982: "In the course of the next decade, nearly every man in that photo would be wounded at least once, some multiple times. Many were maimed or crippled for life. A number would be killed in action." The remainder, he wrote, are "better men for the experience."

Above: Six Sikorsky RH-53D Sea Stallions, the helicopters used to support Delta Force in Operation Eagle Claw

Index

Acknowledgments

We would like to thank the following for the use of their pictures reproduced in the book:

Alamy, 15, 49, 154, 167, 173
Bundesarchiv, Bild 101 I-280-1096-33 / Jacob / CC-BY-SA, 157
Bundesarchiv, Bild 101 III-Gutscher-001-05 / Gutscher / CC-BY-SA, 134
Bundesarchiv, Bild 101 III-Hoffmann-023-11 / Hoffmann / CC-BY-SA, 136
Bundesarchiv, Bild 135-S-05-02-26 / Schäfer, Ernst / CC-BY-SA, 175
Bundesarchiv, Bild 146-1983-108-29 / Woscidlo, Wilfried / CC-BY-SA, 161
Bundesarchiv, Bild 183-H26258 / CC-BY-SA, 158
Bundesarchiv, Bild 183-R99621 / CC-BY-SA, 131
Corbis, cover, 35, 65, 66, 71, 97t/b, 100, 170
Cosma, shutterstock.com, 8 l/r
dkArt, shutterstock.com, 9 r
Getty, 23, 150, 169
Haung Zheng, shutterstock.com, 137
LA(Phot) Dave Hillhouse/MOD, 121
LA(Phot) Si Ethell/MOD, 127
Mary Evans, 47, 73, 135, 147
Marie Lan-Nguyen, 114
Michael G. Smith, shutterstock.com, 2
POA(Phot) Dave Husbands/MOD, 125
POA(Phot) Sean Clee/MOD, 128
SAC Neil Chapman (RAF)/MOD, 179
Sailko, 58r
Sharon Mollerus, 17
Sibrikov Valery, shutterstock.com, 9 l
Staff Sgt. Russell Klika, 184
Olemac, Shutterstock.com, 137
Wikipedia, 11, 12 t/b, 13, 14, 16, 18, 19, 21, 22, 25, 26, 27, 29, 30, 31 l/r, 33, 34, 37, 39, 4ot/b, 41, 42, 43, 44, 45, 48, 50, 52 55, 56, 58l, 59, 60, 61, 63 64, 67, 68, 69, 70, 74, 75, 76, 77t, 81, 82, 85, 90t, 91 t/b, 92, 93, 98, 101, 103, 104, 106, 108 t/b, 110, 112, 113, 115, 116, 117, 122 t/b 123, 126, 132 t/b, 133, 140, 142, 143, 144, 145, 149, 151, 152 t/b, 153, 159, 160, 162-3, 165, 166, 168, 175, 176, 180, 181,182, 183, 185, 187, 188, 189, 191, 193, 195, 196 l/r, 197, 198, 201, 202, 203, 206, 205, 207 208, 209, 211, 212, 213, 214-215, 216, 219

While every effort has been made to credit contributors, the publisher would like to apologize should there have been any omissions or errors and would be pleased to make the appropriate correction for future editions of the book.